THE NEXT
CHRISTIAN FAITH

THE NEXT
CHRISTIAN FAITH

A Brief Sketch

CHRIS KUGLER

CASCADE *Books* • Eugene, Oregon

THE NEXT CHRISTIAN FAITH
A Brief Sketch

Cascade Books
An Imprint of Wipf and Stock Publishers
199 W. 8th Ave., Suite 3
Eugene, OR 97401

www.wipfandstock.com

PAPERBACK ISBN: 978-1-7252-7493-8
HARDCOVER ISBN: 978-1-7252-7494-5
EBOOK ISBN: 978-1-7252-7495-2

Cataloguing-in-Publication data:

Names: Kugler, Chris.

Title: The Next Christian Faith : A Brief Sketch / Chris Kugler.

Description: Eugene, OR: Cascade Books, 2021 | Includes
bibliographical references.

Identifiers: ISBN 978-1-7252-7493-8 (paperback) | ISBN 978-1-7252-
7494-5 (hardcover) | ISBN 978-1-7252-7495-2 (ebook)

Subjects: LCSH: Bible—Criticism, Narrative. | Jesus Christ. | Bible—
Hermenutics.

Classification: BS476 .K80 2021 (paperback) | BS476 (ebook)

02/08/21

To Litty,
who's always known the way.

To Eli,
who's already taken his first steps.

To Brady,
who knows it in his mama's bones.

To Hank,
who often goes before us.

Contents

Preface

THE *NEXT* CHRISTIAN FAITH . . . ?

Really? Isn't that kind of "over the top" . . . kind of dramatic . . . kind of, perhaps, arrogant?

After all, for a movement that began roughly 2,000 years ago and that has, notwithstanding its obvious failings, persisted and contributed much to many different societies throughout that long history, it's quite the claim to hold out the hope/prediction of the *next* Christian faith.

In a sense, I don't intend anything so dramatic, so disjunctive, as the expression "the next Christian faith" might imply. On the other hand, I do intend to indicate that the Christian faith faces many serious—and, indeed, to many strategists, insuperable—challenges. And it is to these that this book is addressed.

In this regard, what I'm attempting to sketch is a Christian "worldview"—an entire way of *being* in the world and, particularly, of understanding that *mode* of being—which is grounded in the worldview of Jesus and the earliest Christians and which, therefore and thereby, rebuts, neutralizes, and/or helpfully recontextualizes the sharper challenges presently facing the Christian faith. As will become obvious, the challenges I have in mind are especially pressing for the contemporary Western world (western Europe and North America), though they are felt elsewhere and increasingly so.

But what are these challenges and how did they come about? (1) Sometime in the second century CE, the church fundamentally lost touch with the Jewish and especially "storied" worldview within which the Bible, and not least its key character, were designed to make sense. (2) Relatedly, as the church became increasingly influenced by non-Jews and by the Greek philosophical tradition (not that this was all bad!), an earlier emphasis upon what we might call "orthomythology" (telling and living within the right *story*) was replaced by an emphasis upon intellectual "orthodoxy" (assenting to the right beliefs). Now, to be crystal clear, of course the earliest Christians held to certain key beliefs without which one would not and could not be a Christian. However, these beliefs meant what they meant *within a presupposed story, a larger narrative concerning "what the world is all about."*

(3) To state it bluntly, most contemporary Christians have misunderstood the nature, shape, and purpose of the Bible.[1] (4) Furthermore, many have lost sight of what the church *is*: its nature, inner logic, and location within the larger biblical vision. (5) In relation to point (4), many have forgotten the political vision of the kingdom of God, the church's role within it, and the way in which this vision upstages the unhelpful (and basically uninteresting) antithesis of "conservative" and "liberal."[2] (6) Finally, most of "evangelicalism" has allowed itself to become increasingly sectarian and isolationist, and not least in relation to issues surrounding "faith and science."[3]

Now, as much as the issues listed above have partly generated this volume and are in view throughout, it would be a mistake to imagine that each of them maps neatly onto one of the following chapters. Rather, they are dealt with throughout the book and *en route*. To bracket the issues into discrete sections would have been artificial and would have totally missed the point.

Moreover, this book is divided into two major sections (followed by an appendix). The first section, "Preliminaries," is largely

1. For some helpful approaches to scripture, see e.g. Wright, *Last Word*; McKnight, *Blue Parakeet*; and Kugler and Shepperd, *Reading the Bible Well*.

2. On the Christian faith and politics, see almost anything by Oliver O'Donovan.

3. For a rejection of this antithesis and an inspiring attempt to engage serious scientific questions, see McKnight and Venema, *Adam and the Genome*, and almost anything by William Lane Craig or Alister McGrath.

stage-setting and ground-clearing; it is not, however, simply the "deconstructive" section that is then followed by the "reconstructive" section. Rather, because we're not only talking about the ancient Christian worldview *but also and simultaneously* about the many ways in which this worldview has been understood and misunderstood in various times and places throughout the last 2,000 years, any negative analysis (deconstruction) is always implicitly constructive and any positive proposal (construction) is always implicitly deconstructive.

The first section ("Preliminaries"), therefore, consists of what is sometimes called *Prolegomena* ("things said beforehand")—that is, the absolutely necessary and fundamental philosophical, theological, and historical points that must be accepted and thoroughly appreciated for *any following constructive proposals to be properly understood.*

The second section ("Constructive Proposals"), then, takes the "Preliminaries" for granted and on their basis offers several constructive proposals for central topics of Christian theology and faith. So, that's how it works.

Let's get started.

PRELIMINARIES

How Did We Get Here?[1]

FIRST, WHERE'S "HERE?"

"Here" is a place where most modern people—*and no less modern Christians*—live within a "worldview story" which is not that of Jesus and the earliest Christians.

"But," you might ask, "if it's just a matter of 'story' and not, in other words, of 'theology' and/or 'doctrine,' why's it so important?" It's important because, I suggest, "theology" and "doctrine" mean what they mean *within an implicit and controlling story.*

You may think that you're "neutral," "objective," and "unbiased." You may think that you're just a "blank slate" coming to the text of Scripture. You may think that, actually, you're not operating with some controlling narrative when you make sense of words and concepts like "God," "Jesus," "sin," "salvation," "judgment," "love," "hate," etc., but you'd be wrong.

In fact, "raw data" doesn't actually have what we call "meaning" until it's located within a larger "context of meaning" that is inevitably "storied" in shape.

Let's take an example . . .

You go to a restaurant after a long day of work. The temperature's great; you get a great table; you order a nice drink and a few appetizers. Then you see a sharply dressed businessman rush into the restaurant and take a seat opposite what appears to be his spouse. An argument ensues. You hear only single, muffled words.

---

1. If you want to go much deeper into the kind of thought reflected in this chapter, see especially Taylor, *Secular Age.*

"Late..."

"Angry..."

"Schedule..."

So, what's the "meaning" of the event? What's the "meaning" of the argument? What's the "meaning" of those three words? We all know that, actually, you can't know the "meaning" of the event or of the words *without knowing the story.*

Because *story* is always the context of "meaning."

"Raw data" simply provides the individual component parts that, when construed together in a larger "story," produce what we call "meaning."

So, back to the restaurant. If story is the ultimate and inevitable context of meaning, how can we ever hope to understand what the argument at the restaurant meant?

What we do is to construct a hypothetical story within which the component parts might have meaning.

We construct a narrative-as-hypothesis within which the details might make sense.

"So," you suppose, "let's imagine that the businessman is regularly late to meet with his wife and she's understandably complaining that he's always "late," never on "schedule," and she's very "angry" about it.

But what if just moments later you come by more data—in the form of hearing more muffled words of the conversation—which suggests to you that your hypothetical story doesn't work as well anymore?

"I can't believe they sprung this cheerleading tryout on those busy kids."

"Hmmm," you think to yourself, "was it actually an *argument* that I heard or simply a frustrated exchange?" Could the exchange actually have been about the woman complaining that she's "angry" because, though it was not on the high school "schedule," her daughter's school was holding cheerleading tryouts "late" on a school night? That would of course mean that the three words that you heard earlier, when understood within *this* story, have quite a different meaning and function.[2]

Words, ideas, concepts, and doctrines mean what they mean within controlling stories.

And the problem is that most Christians aren't living within the same worldview story that Jesus and the earliest Christians were living within.

We'll come to their worldview story in chapter six, but for now let's consider the worldview options of most modern Westerners. To consider this, however, we'll need to rehearse a bit of history, grossly over-simplified.

Sometime in the second century CE, Christianity by and large lost touch with the Jewish and especially storied worldview of Jesus and the earliest Christians. In this specific regard, not much changed from the second to the fifteenth century.[3] So, for our very limited purposes, the fifteenth century's as good a place to pick up the story as any.

The invention of the printing press meant that, compared to earlier times, research and information—not to mention all kinds of literature and poetry—could be widely disseminated and digested at rates and in volumes previously unimaginable. With our computers, iPhones, podcasts, etc., it's hard for us to get a sense of the sheer awe this would have inspired in the general public.

This information revolution precipitated roughly four centuries of unprecedented advancement—at least when compared

---

2. This is not so much a linguistic point about the semantic range of the words in question; rather, it is a point about the way in which isolated pieces of data (in this case, words) don't produce what we call "meaning" until they are gathered together and joined into a "story."

3. I am *not* saying, however, what some modern Protestant theologians and pastors have said: namely, that the church basically went off the rails in ca. 150 CE and didn't get back on the track until the Protestant Reformation (ca. 1517 CE). That's a grossly inaccurate and uncharitable—not to mention theologically problematic—way of conceiving of church history. I'm *only* saying that, rather, Jesus and the earliest Christians—from whom come all of our New Testament authors—saw Scripture and biblical history as one large, multifaceted narrative, whereas this "narrative" and/or "story" approach to Scripture was much less prevalent in the church from ca. 150 CE to the early 20th century.

to the rate of advancement of most earlier times—in the areas of culture, philosophy, science, and technology, just to mention a few areas. This period in Europe from the fifteenth to the eighteenth century comprises what historians call the Renaissance and the Enlightenment.

From the eighteenth to the twenty-first century, technology and medicine would be the face of most of the major developments. The world was, at least from the Western perspective, slowly but surely producing an Edenic universe.

This is the implicit narrative within which many people in our contemporary Western world—our parents or siblings or friends or neighbors—are consciously or subconsciously living.

They're characters in a story, a story about the world, about where it's come from and where it's headed.

And the story goes something like this: before all of this great technology and medicine, we were living in a world of deep darkness. But we're now producing an Edenic universe.

Generally speaking, philosophers and historians refer to this as the "Enlightenment worldview" or some such. And it comes with and presupposes answers to all of the big "worldview" questions:

Q: Where/who is "God?"

A: Who cares? Clearly, at least up to the fifteenth century, if there ever had been a "God," he didn't help us very much. Christianity, for instance, had fifteen centuries to produce Eden and didn't. We can see, therefore, that we're on our own. But, look, we're not doing so bad after all!

Q: What's the point of the universe?

A: I'm not sure, actually. I guess for each of us to build our own tower of Babel as high and sturdy as possible.

Q: Is there anything wrong with the world/you?

A: Yes, but "God" won't fix it. However, if we try really hard, if we can just create the right technology and/or medicine, we can eradicate the world of evil and pain. There's nothing deeper, nothing more fundamentally wrong here.

But, as many others know, however fantastic the advancements of the fifteenth to the twenty-first century, they didn't produce an Edenic universe. Indeed, problems and pain abound. This is, more or less, what philosophers call the "postmodern" reaction to "modernity's" attempts to produce an Edenic universe with all of its technology and medicine.

For these people, the postmodernists, there's not so much a grand macro-story as a deconstruction of story. This is how it goes.

Q: Who/where is "God?"

A: I'm not sure. If there is one, she's clearly impotent and/or cruel.

Q: What's the point of the universe?

A: There isn't one, and as soon as you realize that you'll be better off. Rather, take the concept of a "story for the universe" and transpose that within yourself. The only "story" that matters is your own little and ultimately unredemptive story of "self discovery."

Q: Is there anything wrong with the world/you?

A: Well, probably. But we already know that it can't be fixed. So, simply to cope, we'd be better off redefining "wrong" as "another interesting variation."

These two major worldviews or "macro-stories"—generally conceived—modernity and postmodernity—are the major stories on offer in our contemporary Western world. People construe their entire lives in relation to them.

And the problem is this:

Christianity *itself* is a worldview, a macro-story.

It's not, in other words, an abstract collection of moral and ethical advice that you might insert into a worldview that you got from somewhere else.

And, as we've already seen, *the story makes the meaning.*

You can't serve two masters.

You can't have two controlling stories.

Right-Brain Solutions
for a Left-Brain World[1]

THE BIGGEST CHALLENGE TWENTY-FIRST century people will face when they attempt to inhabit a first-century Christian worldview is this: they're fundamentally programmed not to understand it. In his seminal book, *The Master and His Emissary: The Divided Brain and the Making of the Western World*, psychiatrist Iain McGilchrist persuasively argued that (to oversimplify) "left-brain (left-hemisphere) thinking" has become the dominant mode of thinking in the Western world. Characteristically (again to oversimplify), the left hemisphere of the brain isn't that interested in stories, in larger units of meaning within which isolated facts have the sense they were intended to have. It isn't interested in poetry, prayer, and music. Indeed, the brass-tacks usefulness of these activities is far from apparent to the left hemisphere.

While the left hemisphere of the brain is well suited to analyze small bits of data, to dissect facts and so on, it's not only incapable of making sense of larger units of meaning—of perceiving and operating within larger "narratives" and "stories"—*it's hardly aware that they exist.*

And the problem here is that, as McGilchrist shows, we'd actually be much better off if the right hemisphere were in charge. This hemisphere sees the whole picture and the relationship of its

1. For this whole section, I'm particularly indebted to McGilchrist, *Master and His Emissary.*

constituent parts. This hemisphere, unlike its counterpart, sees the power and utility of the other hemisphere and is happy to cooperate. Indeed, the right hemisphere readily recognizes the superior prowess of the left hemisphere when it comes to many tasks. However, the left hemisphere—quite literally in terms of the way in which the two hemispheres share "information" *via* "commissures"—doesn't see the point of the right hemisphere. Actually, it seems to think that it doesn't need it. After all, what is the ultimate utility of poetry and prayer, of metaphors and music? What is the value of a worldview or a controlling narrative? Does this actually allow us to see the greater meaning of life? Indeed, *is* there a greater meaning?

But what's so concerning about this state of affairs is that it's not just that certain individuals can become "left-brain dominant" but so can *entire cultures*. And the church proves, again and again, to be no exception.

So, if we're ever to understand, let alone to inhabit, a first-century Christian worldview, we must rediscover the depth, beauty, and purpose of the right hemisphere and not least the "categories" with which it likes to work. There's no doubt, for instance, that when reading Scripture the left hemisphere will spot all sorts of specific and important details. But it's the right hemisphere, generally speaking, that's going to help you to make sense of the poetry, the psalmody, the parables, the apocalyptic, and the overall narrative shape.

And again it's that last category—narrative—that is so important; and it's precisely this category that left-hemisphere-dominant folks are least likely to appreciate. But it's so important to remember that the early Christians, like Jesus himself, didn't operate with abstract or systematic categories about "God," "humanity," "sin," "salvation," "judgment," "predestination," "free will," "ethics," etc.

The early Christians, like Jesus himself, believed themselves to be living at a climactic moment within a much larger *story*.

And it's the story that counts.

To History We Must Go

CHRISTIANS NEED HISTORY. THE incarnation—the doctrine that the Second Person of the Trinity, God the Son, became human in and as the first-century Jew Jesus of Nazareth—*demands* that Christians care about history. If the Son of God only *seemed* to be human, but actually wasn't, then we don't need to bother with history too much. If this were the case, then God only *seemed* to reveal himself in and as the first-century Jew Jesus of Nazareth. Again, if this were the case, then God isn't decisively unveiled in and as Jesus, but he only *seems* to be unveiled in and as Jesus. And, actually, if this were the case, then "God" is wholly knowable without much reference to Jesus, *and many Christians in fact live as though this were the case.*

The incarnation, however, *theologically* commits us to history. To put it another way, if God revealed himself in and as the first-century Jew Jesus of Nazareth—as *every* Christian tradition has *always* claimed—then we are ineluctably committed to understanding that first-century revelation. A Christian cannot simultaneously claim to care deeply about the Christian God and not to care too much about the first-century world. After all, Christianity is not a particular philosophy or abstract ethic. It is, rather, about devotion to a God revealed in and as a first-century human being. Therefore, inattention to the first-century humanity of Jesus of Nazareth is inattention to the very self-revelation of God.

Some will no doubt protest that they "know" God and know very little about the Bible and/or about the first century. I don't doubt that this is sometimes the case and, from the perspective of the Christian faith, isn't a problem. Of course, the Holy Spirit might reveal the genuine person and character of Jesus to whomever he sees fit, irrespective of the particulars of Jesus' historical life. I would never deny that God reveals himself clearly to those who call upon him, not least by the presence of the Spirit, both personally and corporately. There are plenty of biblical scholars and theologians who, in that sense, don't "know" Jesus very well. On the other hand, there are plenty of people who know very little about the "historical Jesus" and who, in a different sense, clearly "know" Jesus very well.

However, this does not absolve us of the responsibility of allowing the *historical person of Jesus* to critique and to challenge our potentially self-serving and idolatrous depictions of him. We all know people who say that they "know" Jesus but clearly and unambiguously live for this "Jesus" and talk about this "Jesus" in ways which are totally inconsonant with the depiction of Jesus in the New Testament. Are we simply to say, "Well, he or she 'knows' Jesus. So that 'knowledge' trumps the revelation of the Jesus of the Gospels?"

Perhaps at this point someone will offer a postmodern challenge: "How can we 'know' what the Gospels are actually saying? Aren't we all biased? Aren't we all prone to force the evidence into the service of our own particular agendas?" The post-postmodern Christian responds: "Well, yes, of course, we all see *from our point of view*. There's no escaping that. This is why we do our thinking and our 'knowing' *in public and in dialogue with others*—particularly with those with whom we're prone to disagree—so that our potentially self-serving and idolatrous depictions of Jesus can be shown to be just that. This is, after all, part of the point of a diverse church. If we're all prone to be biased, *then let's get as many potential biases in the room as possible!* However, it's also worth remembering that, though bias is inevitable, it's also *a matter of degree*. The goal is to think *together* and *in public* and to attempt to articulate as unbiased a picture as possible."

However, even in the light of this post-postmodern response, it could be that this kind of "knowledge" is little more than the mean of opinions in a given room. What we actually need is evidence that *pushes back against us and won't allow for easy manipulation.*

11

And that's precisely the place that, in a rich and dense Christian worldview, the Bible (along with "tradition"[1]) assumes. The Bible is a *public* document (documents, actually). It's not, in other words, the private property of some esoteric religion. It's a collection of public documents that, particularly in the case of the four Gospels (Matthew, Mark, Luke, and John), purport to tell the truth about events which actually happened in space-and-time history. The Bible, therefore, does not take us *away* from history but, rather, *to* it.

And for this very reason, the Bible invites—rather than avoids—public discourse and debate: what about the historicity of the Bible?; did Jesus really exist?; can we actually believe in miracles?; what about the resurrection? There's no escaping these questions and withdrawing into some private religious bubble. That route ultimately leads to a rejection of the incarnation.

After all, God himself entered history.

He was not afraid of it.

He engaged it.

He was crucified in it.

And he then and thereby buried it, raised it, and redirected it toward the new world that he is already bringing forth.

---

1. See the next few pages and the next footnote on "tradition."

Starting with Jesus

BUT IF THE INCARNATION stands at the very heart of the Christian faith, this has massive implications for how we think about, and live within, this faith.

We *begin* with Jesus.

We don't start with our favorite doctrines. We don't start with the creeds. We don't even, *as a matter of theological principle*, start with Scripture. Nor do we start with some vague conception of "God," as though this figure were somehow knowable *before we knew anything about Jesus.*

No.

The New Testament is clear: we *start* with Jesus. It is *through Jesus* that we discover the meaning of the word "God."

However, haven't I just contradicted myself? Didn't I just say: "*the New Testament* is clear?" Haven't I, therefore, begun with *Scripture?*

Well, in a sense.

But if I start with the New Testament, haven't I begun with church "tradition," as the canon was originally demarcated by the early church?

Well, in a sense.

And why would I start with the church's canon unless I'd already come to the conclusion that the Spirit was at work in the church, guiding it properly to demarcate the inspired canon? Haven't I, therefore, *actually* begun with the Spirit?

Well, in a sense.

And why would I begin with the Spirit unless I'd already decided to accord theological authority to my own personal experience of the Spirit?

Scripture; tradition; reason; experience.[1]

That's actually how all knowledge works. "Scripture" stands in for "evidence/data." "Tradition" stands in for the rich history of intelligent engagement with the "evidence/data." "Reason" represents the ordinary canons of rationality (noncontradiction and so on). And "experience" refers to the totality of the "contact" which an entire embodied, embedded, and located human being has with all of reality.[2]

There's nothing distinctively Christian/spiritual/religious about this (very briefly articulated) "epistemology" (theory of how we know things). Christians should not base their worldview on special pleading. We shouldn't say: "Well, *our* worldview, and *our* theory of knowledge that sustains it, is completely detached and unrelated to other widely held theories of how we know things. We take it, in other words, on *faith*."

This is the way, I suggest, to an un-Christian, anticreational worldview. Rather, mainstream Christianity claims, and has always claimed, that God made, sustains, and loves this *good* if broken world. Mainstream Christianity claims, and has always claimed, that God himself *united* himself to this world once and for all and forever in the person of his Son, Jesus of Nazareth. In other words, although Christianity has always postulated that this world is fundamentally broken—a brokenness that has inevitable effects on our "knowing"—it does not postulate that "ordinary human knowing" is problematic.

To this picture, however, I should add a crucial caveat. Christianity has always claimed that, because of the fundamental brokenness of this world and of human beings within it, a proper

---

1. This is, of course, the Wesleyan Quadrilateral.

2. In their different ways, both Dreyfus and Taylor, *Retrieving Realism*, and Hart, *Being, Consciousness, Bliss*, make a compelling case for the proper role of what we call "experience"—in Dreyfus and Taylor's language it is the totality of "primal contact" we have with reality—in an overall epistemology. Hereby they challenge the skeptical, Cartesian tradition of internalism and reductionism.

worldview can only be attained because of and after the saving work of God's Spirit. In other words, from Christianity's perspective, it is impossible to have a proper worldview before and apart from the rescuing activity of God's Spirit.

But this emphatically doesn't mean that, in light of and after one's experience of God, such a person's worldview represents such a radical break with "ordinary ways of knowing" that they then reject the place of "evidence/data" (Scripture); "the history of intelligent engagement with the evidence/data" (tradition); and "ordinary and widely accepted canons of rationality" (reason).

So, following this long and complex aside, we come back to the point: a Christian worldview *begins with Jesus*.

But the above aside was necessary to establish the dialectical nature of Christian knowing. We need (Spirit-inspired and -sustained) experience, which prompts us to accord all and supreme theological authority to God incarnate (the *historical* person of Jesus of Nazareth), whose supreme authority is conveyed by the derivative (but nonetheless *real*) authority of Scripture and secondarily tradition's organic and faithful appropriation of Scripture, all of which forms a worldview which is "reasonable."

Scripture; tradition; reason; experience.

Nevertheless, as a theological principle, it is the historical person of Jesus himself—God enfleshed in and as a real historical person—whose theological authority is primary and supreme, even if and though that authority is ultimately (and properly) mediated by the church's (tradition's) Scripture.[3]

To illustrate this principle, let's look at a few biblical passages:

> [Jesus] is the visible image of the invisible God (Col 1:15 NRSV).

> Long ago God spoke to our ancestors through the prophets in many and various ways, but in these last days he has spoken to us by his son (Heb 1:1–2 NRSV).

---

3. Unless otherwise indicated throughout this book, all scriptural translations are my own.

> No one has ever seen God. But God the only son, who
> was in the bosom of the father, has made him known
> (John 1:18 NRSV).

The New Testament makes the point again and again: if you want to know the true and only God, *you have to look long and hard at Jesus.* Moreover, to take another cue from John, you have to look long and hard at the *historical* Jesus:

> And the Word became flesh and dwelt among us . . .
> (John 1:14 NRSV).[4]

In other words, it won't do to say: "I know Jesus. I feel him strongly in my heart. Whether or not my vague, spiritual conceptions of Jesus correspond to the actual human being who walked in first-century Palestine doesn't really matter." Go that route and you'll discover that, as the church (and I) have discovered again and again, you're worshipping an idol, a Jesus who looks suspiciously like yourself and your own culture. No. We need Jesus himself—the first-century Jew, the human being in whom the Second Person of the Trinity became incarnate—to stand over against us and to show us what the true God is actually like. And when this happens, we discover that the true God came in and as a first-century Jew, and that this God's Jewishness was not incidental. It was and remains a central part of that revelation.

He thought like a Jew. He spoke like a Jew. He acted like a Jew. He constructed his whole life on a vision derived from the Jewish Scriptures.

This is the true God, and he invites us to learn to reinhabit that first-century world, not so that we can escape our own but so that we can reclaim the resources he gave us to rescue it.

"But," many will protest, "I'm not a biblical scholar. I don't know much about ancient history or ancient Judaism. How could I possibly get to know the *historical* Jesus, especially if this involves getting to know *that* world?" To this I'd say several things, all of which require a paragraph of their own.

---

4. On the historical Jesus, see especially Wright, *Challenge of Jesus* and *Simply Jesus.*

We've wrongly imagined that Christian faith is simply and exclusively about what we call "spirituality." In other words, *because the Christian faith is little more than a system designed to facilitate my own inner, spiritual/psychological happiness,* I shouldn't have to spend any time getting to know the context within which the Bible was written. This is a massive mistake. Certainly the Christian faith includes a vision of individual spirituality but it is far from reducible to that vision. Rather, the Christian faith claims to tell the true story *about the whole universe,* a universe which, so this faith claims, reached its climactic moment in events that happened in the first century. To put it bluntly, *you simply can't properly understand those events without knowing certain things about the first century.*

This does *not* mean that you can't know God without a deep understanding of the Bible's ancient context. However, though the Christian tradition has always affirmed that individuals can and do have immediate access to God *via* the Spirit, this is not in itself an argument against the basic New Testament principle that God was and is decisively unveiled in and as a real person of first-century history.

Last of all, I'd say that we have more access to Jesus' world now than ever before. You can easily google fantastic videos and lectures. You have access to audiobooks. All of the relevant material is widely available. For example, just to listen/read one (or all) of these three books would be an extraordinary start:

- McKnight, Scot. *The King Jesus Gospel: The Original Good News Revisited.*

- Wright, N. T. *The Challenge of Jesus: Rediscovering Who Jesus Was and Is.*

- Wright, N. T. *Simply Jesus: A New Vision of Who He Was, What He Did, and Why It Matters.*

Let's now turn to the Bible itself.

The Bible:
What Kind of Book Is This?

WHAT KIND OF "AUTHORITY" is this?

In the Protestant tradition, the Bible comprises sixty-six books and several different genres.[1] We have myths and epics, poems and prayers, songs and semi-biographies, letters and even some apocalyptic literature. How can *this* book be authoritative? And what would this authority look like?

Part of the clue to the way in which the Bible's authority works lies both in the meaning of Jesus' crucifixion and in the nature of the Bible itself.[2]

Let's take the former first. The whole story of the Gospels, of the mission and message of Jesus of Nazareth, involves God's purpose to reassume sovereignty—one might even say authority—over the beloved world that he originally created. As humans worshipped beings other than the true God, and as this thereby gave power to anticreational forces in the world (traditionally referred to as "Satan" and "demons"), God's authority was (in a sense) usurped. That's part of the point of the story of the serpent in Genesis 3. But how did God go about getting back his creation? What was the manner in which he reestablished his authority?

---

1. The Roman Catholic and Eastern Orthodox traditions include a few other fascinating "apocryphal" books in their canons.

2. Some of the connections that follow are scattered throughout Wright, *Last Word*.

Well, first, it's important to remember that this is exactly what Jesus said *he* was doing. When Jesus went about ancient Palestine proclaiming "the gospel of the kingdom of God" (for example, Mark 1:14–15), this is what he was talking about. He was referring to the good news that God was finally establishing his kingdom "on earth as it is in heaven" (Matt 6:10). God was assuming a rescuing and restorative control over his broken creation. So it's no coincidence that this would-be Messiah, this would-be king of Israel and the world, finished his kingdom-bringing work when he was crucified by the most powerful nation on earth (Rome) with this inscription above his head: "Jesus of Nazareth, the *King* of the Jews."

God's authority had come, and it had come in and through the brutal execution of his beloved Son.

The cross and the crown belong together.

But what does *this* say about God's authority?

Let's come at this question from a different angle. What might the nature of the Bible itself tell us about *this* God's authority? What kind of book is this? And what kind of authority can and should we expect *this kind of book* to exercise?

This is clearly not a rule book, an ethics book, or a science book. For example, no matter how hard we try to make the poem of Genesis 1 to function like modern science, it will nevertheless remain an ancient myth about the deepest meaning of existence, of human life, and of God's creative purposes. We're not being "conservative" when we attempt to make the book God gave us into something else. We're not being "faithful." The point is not to assume that we already know what God's authority will look like— "Surely he'll give us *this* kind of book"—and then to make sure that this is indeed the kind of authority the Bible is allowed to exercise. Rather, we have to stare long and hard at Scripture, and not least at Scripture's key character, to discover for the first time what God's authority might look like.

And, at first glance, it appears to look like whatever kind of authority a *story* might have. Story, after all, is the overarching genre of the Bible.

It's a massive and dangerous story about the creator God's purposes for the whole world, purposes put into operation through his human creatures.

But if it's fundamentally a story, does this mean that God doesn't care how we live? In other words, does the Bible have anything to say about what we call "ethics?"

Of course.

But, our abstract notion of "ethics" isn't particularly biblical. In the Bible, the larger category is never a list of moral principles that you need to follow in order to be a better person. Rather, the overarching category is *always* the story of God's purposes to fill the whole creation with justice and beauty and *the kind of human beings he'll need to accomplish this purpose.* I'll put it this way: in the Bible, it's not so much about ethics as it's about becoming the kind of person that can be a protagonist *in this story.*

But how do stories work?

Stories construct the universe. They gather up all the loose and complex details of existence and offer a larger narrative within which they might make sense. Stories slowly but surely draw us into their awesome power. And, perhaps most importantly in this connection, some stories are open-ended, and this is no less the case with Scripture. In this sense, the Bible tells a story which is *unfinished.*

The Bible asks each of us, then: What kind of character are *you* going to be; what role are *you* going to play; based upon the story so far, where do you think this whole thing is headed and *how are you going to ensure that it gets there*?

But if the Bible is fundamentally a story, does this mean that it functions like fiction? Does it matter, in other words, if any of it actually happened?

Now we come to a tricky question, and one that we'll deal with in more detail in a later chapter. Some details matter and some don't. For example, many ancient societies told odd stories about the creation of the universe; many told stories about a massive flood. What matters about *some* of these stories isn't that they accurately depict the material origins of the universe but that they reflect deep and profound truths about the most meaningful questions of existence:

who/what is the divine; what's the point of human existence; what's right and/or wrong with us/the world?; where's this whole thing headed? The genre of these stories is "myth." It is, therefore, a category mistake to ask questions that are inappropriate to the genre, such as, "What breed of snake deceived Adam and Eve?"

But this doesn't mean, of course, that other genres in the Bible aren't concerned with the historicity of the things they narrate. Many of the narratives of the people of Israel come to mind, as does the historical life and ministry of Jesus of Nazareth. These things *happened*, and it matters deeply that they happened.

Here's the point: we're not being faithful to the Bible when we try to make its diverse genres operate in ways for which they weren't originally designed (and inspired).

When we try to make the Bible do something for which it wasn't originally designed, we're not submitting to God's authority but rejecting it.

So, to return to the point, how does the Bible's authority work? We can now join this up with our earlier discussion of the meaning of Jesus' crucifixion. God's authority, in the end, doesn't work in the way we might have expected. He doesn't give rules from a distance. He doesn't offer a grand textbook. Rather, he hangs there on Good Friday, crowned and enthroned, holding auditions for a massive story within which we are called to discover better families, more connected communities, more just and generous societies, and above all that glorious and elusive hope of a genuine humanness. That's how stories work and that's what God gave us.

The Bible:
What Kind of Story Is This?

FOR JESUS AND THE earliest Christians, "truth" in general, and moral/theological truths in particular, meant what they meant within the larger biblical story running from Genesis 1 to Revelation 22: a story of (1) creation (Gen 1–2), (2) fall and brokenness (Gen 3), (3) God's purpose to renew creation through Abraham and his family Israel (Gen 12 through the whole Old Testament), (4) Israel's "fall" into exile, (5) the rescue of Israel and the world brought about by Jesus' life, death, and resurrection (the Gospels), (6) and the vibrant life and vocation of early Christian communities empowered by the Spirit, both instantiating God's new creation in the present and awaiting its consummation at the return of the king himself (the rest of the New Testament).

That's a *story*.

But let's take a closer look.

In the beginning, it's simply taken for granted that there's a "God," whatever that might eventually mean. But it seems to refer to an invisible, immaterial being who, for some reason not stated, created a world of immense beauty and power. This being seems, moreover, to have wanted to accomplish some great purpose in and through human creatures. Indeed, that seems to be part of the point when Genesis states right up front that this God made humans "in his image, according to his likeness" (Gen 1:26). This seems to mean, more or less, that this God wanted human creatures both to represent and to embody his gentle stewardship of the earth.

But where's this story headed?

It pretty much immediately goes wrong.

Without any explanation at all, right in the midst of "and he saw that it was good . . . and he saw that it was good . . . and he saw that it was good," the writer of the first book of the Bible tells us that "the serpent was more crafty than any other wild animal that the LORD God had made" (Gen 3:1 NRSV).

Wait. What?

A serpent? Where did *this thing* come from?

There is no explanation at all—and that in itself is illuminating. The world is, from the perspective of the first three chapters of the Bible, a place of great beauty and power, of goodness and dynamism and creativity. But it's also a place of potential darkness and devastation. Or, rather, it *at some point* became that kind of place.

In any case, what does the serpent basically do? He ultimately tries to persuade human beings to attempt to "become like God" (Gen 3:5). But, if you know the earlier part of the story, the part where God made human beings "in his image, *according to his likeness*" (Gen. 1:26), you see that this is a pretty hollow offer. After all, according to the writer of Genesis, human beings are *already like God*—that is, they already have the closest possible connection with this being. And, in a sense, that is part of the point.

Evil sneaks into God's world and attempts to convince human beings that they aren't what God has already made them, that they don't have what God has already given them.

So that's Genesis 1–3.

From here, we can speed up a bit. There's a flood (Gen 6–9) and this odd tower (Gen 11). Essentially, God's purpose to fill the world with his own creative life in and through human creatures has gone drastically wrong.

So what's this God going to do about it?

The answer to that question begins in Genesis 12 and takes up the rest of the Old Testament.

God will call this man named Abraham and, as Genesis 12:3 puts it, "in you [Abraham] all the families of the earth shall be blessed." In other words, through Abraham and his family (Israel) God is going to rescue the world Adam and Eve got off track.

That is what the whole Bible's about.

God made a covenant with Abraham and his family Israel (Gen 12–22) through which he intended to put the world right again.

Great! But what happens to Abraham's family? What happens to the historical people of Israel?

As book after book and prophet after prophet in the Old Testament say, Israel failed to keep her end of the covenant. Though God intended to rescue the whole world through Israel, Israel too, like Adam and Eve, failed in her vocation.

So what is God going to do now?

Is he going to give up on the project of Genesis 1–2, the divine project to flood the world with creativity, goodness, justice, and peace in and through human creatures?

If not, is he at least going to give up on his covenant with Israel through which he intended to get that project back on track?

No.

The New Testament is emphatic: Jesus is God's true Adam; Jesus is God's true Israel.

Jesus is God's "Yes" to Israel's covenant and thereby to God's creation (2 Cor 1:20).

If you miss this, then you'll miss the logic of the whole New Testament. God intended to steward the world through human beings made in his image. When Adam and Eve rejected this vocation, God called Abraham's family—another group of human beings—to be his means of rescuing the now-broken world. When Abraham's family, Israel, failed in their vocation, *God didn't and wouldn't give up on his age-old purpose of stewarding and now rescuing the world in and through a human being.*

That's the logic of the incarnation.

The incarnation is what happens when the indomitable purpose of God meets the universal infidelity of human creatures.

God himself must come in and as a human being, in and as Adam, in and as Israel, in and as Jesus of Nazareth.

And it's from this vantage point alone—the vantage point provided by the large, multilayered biblical story—that we can see the aims and intentions of Jesus for the first time. What exactly, after all, was Jesus *doing*? What are, in other words, the four Gospels all about?

Matthew and Luke, in their very different ways, begin with the famous birth stories. Jesus' origins, they are saying, lie somewhere else, somewhere mysterious, somewhere "beyond." Jesus' arrival, they are saying, marks a great moment—indeed, *the great moment*—in God's purposes for the whole world.

It comes with all the glory and potential of God's first creation; it comes with all the healing and hope of God's new creation.

John, too, in his own way, tells us that Jesus' origins, as the "Word" (John 1:1–18), lie in the very heart of the one creator God himself (John 1:18). But this same Word, so John also tells us (John 1:14), became wholly and fully human.

Mark, somewhat more dramatically than the others, indicates that this Jesus came to face off against evil and once and for all to defeat it. Jesus' real enemy, Mark wants us to know, is that mysterious dark force that lies behind and energizes human evil.

Notwithstanding the many fascinating differences between the four Gospels, they each tell the same story. This Jesus' origins lie, somehow and mysteriously, before the creation of the world with, in, and as the one true God himself. And this God shows up with skin on—made up, just like you and me, of flesh and blood.

But what did Jesus say and what did Jesus do? Or, to put it differently, what was his life all about? Again, the Gospels are more or less in agreement. This Jesus launched a kingdom of God movement (see especially Matt 3:2; 6:10; Mark 1:15; Luke 4:43; John 3:3–5) in which, by the power of the Spirit, he announced, embodied, and enacted the reestablishment of God's good sovereignty over Israel and the world, symbolized and effected by his calling of twelve disciples (evoking the twelve tribes of Israel), his preaching and teaching, his healings and exorcisms, his acts of power and service, and particularly his evil-defeating death and resurrection.

Jesus understood himself to be the meeting place of heaven and earth, of God's creation project and Adam's vocation, of God's covenantal purpose and Israel's necessary faithfulness, of God's saving justice and the world's deep evil.

Jesus would get God's creation project—the project launched in Genesis 1–2—back on track.

God would get on the cross what he'd been looking for in the garden: a human being embodying *his kind* of sovereignty over the whole world.

That is, in sum, what Jesus was and is all about.

But, according to the New Testament, what did Jesus' life, death, and resurrection accomplish? What, in other words, is Easter all about? Again, in all four Gospels, the point is that God's creation project is back on track. John gets it exactly right.

"Now there was a garden in the place where he was crucified . . ." (John 19:41 NRSV).

And on Easter morning, when Mary Magdalene came to the garden tomb, she saw the risen Jesus but "supposed him to be the gardener" (John 20:15).

And she wasn't wrong.

Jesus is God and Adam in person, God and Israel in person, reclaiming his creation project.

The garden is replanted. Eden is reestablished. God doesn't give up on his purpose to fill the world with justice and peace *in and through his human creatures.*

But where are we now? Where is *Jesus* now? What's the present plot and what happens next? We could put the question this way: What's the point of the odd Christian idea that Jesus would come *twice*? He came once, apparently, to rescue the world through his incarnation, death, and resurrection. He will come again, apparently, to complete his work fully.

But why didn't he do that the first time? Why didn't Jesus, in one fell swoop, fix all of the problems of the world when he first came?

We could put it this way: What's the point of the two comings of Jesus, on the one hand, and of the outpouring of the Holy Spirit (Acts 2), on the other?

The point seems to be that *this* God doesn't intend to fix the problems of the world on his own.

Rather, this God intends to energize genuine human beings in and through whose loving wisdom and sacrificial service the world will be filled with God's own healing and sustaining life.

Now, to be clear, I do not imagine that, to put it bluntly, the church will simply establish paradise on earth. In this regard, the church has oscillated between two extreme and unhelpful positions.

On the one hand, many have imagined that, despite Jesus' rescuing work when he came the first time, and despite the gift of the Holy Spirit in and through the church, the world will nevertheless get worse and worse until Jesus comes back to reverse the whole mess. This view often completely misses the point of Jesus' saving work and of the outpouring of his Spirit.

On the other hand, some Christians have imagined that, given enough time and prayer and ministry, we'll simply discover one day that, in fact, we have fully planted Eden underneath our own noses and without even noticing. This view, I think, underestimates just how broken our world is.

Rather, the biblical vision is somewhere in between these two extremes.

The analogy of a party might prove helpful.

Jesus' incarnation, death, and resurrection, along with the outpouring of his Spirit, liberates human beings from their enslavement, from their various forms of imprisonment. That rescue is once and for all and forever, decisive and unrepeatable.

However, imagine that Jesus rescues these human beings precisely in view of the day when they will throw a party at his return, a party in which the whole universe will take joyous part. Imagine that Jesus had *this* in mind when he rescued these human beings (see Matt 8:11 and Mark 14:25).

Now, everybody loves a party, but nobody wants to throw their own. Rather, they want their closest family and friends to set up the party, to make the arrangements, to plan the activities and decorations and even some surprises!

That's the role of the people rescued from their various forms of slavery and empowered by the Spirit.

PRELIMINARIES

They couldn't plan the party without first being rescued. And Jesus won't throw his own party. However, neither will the party be in full swing simply with the preparations and arrangements.

The one whose party it is must finally show up.

The Church

For Jason, who loves the church.

BUT WHAT MIGHT ALL of this mean for the life of the church? Let me be clear right up front: I spend most of my time studying Scripture and its ancient context. I don't have any particularly strong experience in pastoral ministry, organizational development and management, the facilitation of large and small groups, counseling, and the many other tasks of the church leader. So, there's no doubt that some folks with experience in the above areas will read the next few pages and think: "Well, that *sounds* nice but this guy clearly hasn't considered the particular challenges of [this] and [that]." That's fair. In what follows, therefore, I'm offering large and general reflections about what the church *is* in the Bible. How to work this out in specific cases and specific cultures is the very challenging and exciting task of others.

We now turn to the Bible's vision of the church; and this vision is, as we've now come to expect, storied in shape. It goes something like this.

The one God had a purpose to flood the world with his own dynamic and creative life in and through human beings. That's the point of Genesis 1–2. When this project got off track (Gen 3–11), God remained faithful to his purpose. He called a subset of human beings—Abraham and his family (the people of Israel)—to be his means of stewarding and now redeeming the broken human race and (as a result of the latter) the broken world. And when Israel was unfaithful to the covenant—the very covenant designed to accomplish God's saving purposes—God himself remained faithful. He condemned humanity's faithlessness in general and Israel's faithlessness in particular in the person of Jesus the Messiah.

Here's how this worked. In the first century CE, the people of Israel were under a "covenant curse." What this basically means is that Israel had decisively broken her covenant with God and that this covenant could not be renewed without a decisive act of God. What God required in general was a faithful human being through whom he could accomplish his purposes. What God required in particular was a faithful human *Israelite* through whom (and *as whom*) he could accomplish his purposes.

So God came, the whole New Testament tells us, in and as the one historical person Jesus of Nazareth. This Jesus would be the person in and as whom God would establish his healing and restorative kingdom on earth as it is in heaven.

God would finally steward his beloved creation in and through (and, in this one unique case, *as*) a human being.

God would condemn the sin because of which humans (and the world) were broken.

God would condemn the covenant faithlessness because of which Israel was under a "covenant curse."

God himself, in and as Jesus, would gather up the sinfulness of the whole world onto himself, decisively dealing with it there, once and for all.

However, slowly but surely, this Jesus drew to himself a large gathering of people. More particularly, he was remembered to have gathered to himself twelve Jewish disciples. Doubtless this was a graphic symbol for the restoration of the people (the twelve tribes) of Israel, the people called both to assume Adam's original position over the creation and to rescue him. Jesus, thus, in his life, death, resurrection, ascension, and the outpouring of his Spirit, was reinstantiating the people of God.

But, and this is crucial to say at this point, the church doesn't "replace" Israel.

Here are the several ways in which Paul puts this in his letter to the Romans:

- "Will their faithlessness nullify the faithfulness of God? *By no means!*" (Rom 3:3–4).

- "Has God rejected his people? *By no means!*" (Rom 11:1).

- "For the gifts and the calling of God are *irrevocable*" (Rom 11:29).

Nor is it the case, however, as many people have imagined, that God now has the equivalent of two covenants: one with the ethnic people of Israel, regardless of their allegiance to Jesus the Messiah, and one with non-Jews on the basis of their faith in Jesus.

Rather, as Paul says: "For being a Jew is not a matter of appearances [ethnicity, circumcision, kosher laws, and Sabbath observance], nor does circumcision consist of something physical in the flesh; but Jewishness is hidden, and circumcision is effected by the Spirit in the heart; it's not something physical" (Rom 2:28–29).

So how does this work?

God has not rejected his people. God will remain faithful to his promises to rescue the world in and through Israel in general and in and through Israel's Messiah in particular. As Paul says in Romans 3:22, "Now, the covenant faithfulness of God has been unveiled through the faithfulness of Jesus the Messiah for the benefit of all who are also faithful."

Do you see how it works?

God has been faithful to his covenantal promises to rescue Israel and to rescue the world through Israel *through Jesus, Israel's representative Messiah*. The phrase "God's righteousness" (in Greek: *dikaiosynē theou*), which I translate as "God's covenant faithfulness," denotes the way in which God has upheld his end of the covenant promises; in other words, he is "in the right" (righteous) with respect to his end of the covenant. A covenant is, after all, a *legal* agreement. To be "righteous" in this sense means that one has upheld his or her end of the agreement. God *has been* faithful. Israel, on the other hand, *has not* been faithful.

So here's the pinch—and this is the key to the letter to the Romans (and actually to so much else): How is God going to remain faithful to his purpose to steward the world through human beings and now—because of human sinfulness—to deal with human sinfulness and then to forward his purpose of stewarding the world through human beings?

After all, the very mechanism of this purpose was the covenant with Israel.

And Israel has been unfaithful to the covenant.

That's why Paul asks the question: "Hasn't their faithlessness nullified the faithfulness of God?" (Rom 3:3).

In other words, doesn't one party's unfaithfulness to an agreement jeopardize the goal of the agreement itself? In this specific instance, the point is: *Doesn't Israel's unfaithfulness mean that human beings and the whole world will remain in ruins and God's creation project will never get back on track?*

It is to this dire situation that Paul responds with: "Now, the covenant faithfulness of God has been unveiled through the faithfulness of Jesus the Messiah for the benefit of all who are also faithful" (Rom 3:22).

In other words, the whole purpose of God—to establish human beings as his means of stewarding the world; to be faithful to this purpose in and through Israel; to deal with sin and to rescue humans back to the position of purpose for which they were originally destined—has devolved onto Jesus, Adam, and Israel in person. And don't miss it: this is *for the benefit of all*.

In other words, in Jesus, God has dealt with that which kept human beings and the whole world in a state of brokenness; or, to put it differently, because Jesus' death and resurrection accomplished the forgiveness of the universe and of all human beings within it, and because his outpoured Spirit offers the very real prospect of a renewed and genuine humanness, *the project which God launched in Genesis 1–2 can now finally get back on track.*

That's how it works.

But who are the people through whom God has now launched this project of *new creation*? Our phrase for this group, for the transhistorical, transethnic, transcultural, and transnational family of all those in Israel's Messiah, Jesus, is "the church." And it is from this vantage point alone that we can finally glimpse the purpose, nature, and shape of this new family.

No one has "replaced" Israel. From the beginning, God wanted a multiethnic, multicultural, and multinational family through whom he could steward the ongoing creation of his world. This went drastically wrong. God, therefore, called a subset of human beings—Israel—not to *replace* the human race, nor to *replace* his project of stewarding the ongoing creation of the world through a diverse, world-wide family, but precisely to be his means of bringing that family into being! That is the whole point of Jesus' life, death, resurrection, and the outpouring of his Spirit.

The covenant people of God narrows to Jesus himself, Israel's representative Messiah, and then widens to include all of his earliest Jewish followers and then wider to include *all those in the Messiah*.

This is Israel.

Where Jesus is, Israel is.

But what does this have to do with the contemporary church?

As I've emphasized throughout, everything has its meaning within a story. And, in this case, the church means what it means *within this story and not some other*.

In other words, the church plays a particular role at a particular point in a particular narrative. (1) God intended to imagine a world into existence in and through the creative imagination of his human creatures; (2) Adam and Eve rejected this vocation; (3) God intended to get this project back on track in and through Abraham and his family; (4) God was faithful to his purpose in and through Abraham's family—both to rescue them and to rescue the world through them—in and as Israel's representative Messiah, Jesus. Hereby, God put the creation project of Genesis 1–2 back on track. (5) On the basis of Jesus' death and resurrection and the outpouring of his Spirit, the Jew-plus-gentile people of God in the Messiah are God's new and true humanity, the Adams and Eves through whom God now intends to forward his creation project, to plant his new world.

That's what the church *is*.

We are the people called to pray long and hard into God's original intention for the universe; to worship long and hard into the one God's self-revelation in and as Jesus; to orient ourselves within *this* big story; to imagine ahead to where God wants this whole thing to go; and, crucially, in our individual Christian communities and in our individual lives both to instantiate and to anticipate God's new world, a world where heaven and earth are joined once and for all.

But what difference should any of this make to the ways in which we think about and actually *do* church?

What are we doing when we *do* church?

What's this thing all about?

What are these people all about?

Where'd we come from?

Where are we headed?

The church is a place where heaven and earth have, in some decisive sense, already come together.

The church is the *locus* of God's new world in the present, God's new humanity ahead of the resurrection.

And the church is, particularly, to pick up an analogy from earlier, planning and in a sense already celebrating the coming party, putting up the decorations and already playing the music.

So the church must constantly ask itself: What is God's new world going to be like? What *should* God's new world be like?

That's the dangerous and exploratory part. God's not simply going to tell us. There's no road map. But it probably looks something like magnificent landscapes and cityscapes, meaning and purpose, rest and work, love and joy, sweat and worship, new challenges and new tasks.

It looks like colors and food, music and dancing.

It looks like the last are first and the first are last.

It looks like architecture and agriculture, exploration and reflection.

It looks like the garden of Eden.

And over it all hangs the glorious Lamb, whose cross planted God's new world.

And in the middle of it all walks the Lion of the tribe of Judah.

And suffusing it through and through is the joyous and creative life of the Spirit of the one God.

So church is a place where we tell the big story; we preach the big story; we pray within and into the big story; we sing about the big story; and we invite others into the big story.

And it's especially a place where we're asking all the time: if our church and/or community is like *this* and we know that God's new world is going to be like *that*, how can we make *this* a little more like *that*?

And we don't just believe it; we *try* it.

Excursus: The Church and Politics

THIS BOOK WOULD FEEL incomplete—as does any account of the gospel—without a brief discussion of the relationship between the Christian worldview and what we call "politics."

In this regard, it's crucial to understand that Christianity is neither apolitical nor simply political (at least in the modern sense) but "supra-political." That is, it's a larger construal of the whole of life within which the smaller categories of, for example, "politics," "ethics," and "spirituality" were designed to make sense. But simply because Christianity is not *reducible* to a particular modern sociopolitical vision does not mean that the Christian worldview does not contain a major sociopolitical component.

The Christian God cares about *this* world.

And he cares about the way in which this world works.

So the question isn't, "Does the Christian faith have political implications?," but "What *are* the political implications of the Christian faith?"

In what follows, I intend to paint with very broad, but hopefully helpful, brushstrokes.

Was it a good thing that Christianity eventually became a "state religion" under Constantine (323 CE)?

Was it good either for the church or for the state?

Should there be a separation of church and state? If so, why?

Is it actually possible to have a "neutral" worldview by which to govern?

The previous questions are not easy to answer and certainly not by a nonexpert in a few pages. So, what I hope to offer here are some general guidelines to keep us from two unhelpful extremes.

Is the Christian faith apolitical? Christians who take this position usually do so because of a major misreading of Scripture. It goes something like this.

Because Christianity—like all other "religions"—is *really* about an otherworldly, heavenly communion with the divine, and because, therefore, our materially and historically located human lives, vocations, cultures, and sociopolitical contexts are temporary and apparently unmeaningful in the eternal/spiritual sense, Christians can largely ignore them. Because, so this line of reasoning goes, this world of materiality, of humans and cultures and societies and cities, is simply the "test tube" within which God performed the experiment of seeing who would love him and who wouldn't, we don't have to worry too much about the significance/meaning of the test tube.

But let's say that this more reflects ancient Greek dualism than biblical Christianity, the former of which regarded the created order as a lesser form of existence from which we must ultimately escape, and the latter of which regarded the created order as an ultimate good that was to be redeemed. If so, an altogether different perspective emerges.

Let's say that most Christian visions of the future are far too disjunctive, imagining that the Spirit-inspired church actually accomplishes very little as the world gets worse and worse until Jesus returns to clean up the whole mess.

Let's say that, on the other hand, the world of materiality, of culture and politics, is essentially a good if deeply distorted, corrupted, and broken thing.

Let's say that, actually, being made in God's image and likeness (Gen 1:26-28) is unavoidably "political" insofar as it involves working toward the every-dimensional goodness of God's created world, a pursuit which quickly breaks out of personal ethics and into the worlds of family life, church life, city, state, and global life.

And then let's say that the church is the community being renewed according to the image of God's son, Jesus (Col 3:10), and that, therefore, part of the whole point of the church is to be the community in which and through which God is bringing his new way of ordering the world into being.

So, while it's not always clear whom you should vote for, which party you should support, and so on, the following is pretty clear:

1. Sectarian isolationism isn't Christian—"washing our hands" of the world, withdrawing to the side, and insisting upon our personal holiness.
2. Nationalism isn't Christian. It's obviously fine to celebrate what can and should be celebrated about one's own country; however, it's *not* okay to forget that Christianity is a *transnational*, universal vision about *all of humanity and all of God's creation*.
3. Petty partisanship isn't Christian. We must never fail to distinguish between modern political visions and the ancient, biblical vision of early Christianity.
4. Any political and/or economic visions which do not feature a cross—i.e., some kind of serious, sacrificial component—are not Christian.

The way of Jesus rejects both Christian isolationism and Christian nationalism, and it has little time for the naïve, post-Enlightenment attempt to articulate a political vision in a supposed vacuum, a vision somehow isolated from and constructed without reference to theological and philosophical traditions.

To the post-Enlightenment secularist, the Christian tradition says: "No worldview is neutral. We're always operating on the basis of a metaphysic (belief in, or rejection of, the divine) and a philosophy of morality. They all ultimately derive from somewhere. So let's do one another a favor and drop the 'neutral' and 'objective' language."

And to the "Christian" nationalist the Christian tradition responds: "God's aim is to flood the whole universe—with its many-splendored diversity—with his beautiful and divine life, not simply one particular country."

Likewise, to the Christian isolationist, the Christian tradition responds: "Jesus of Nazareth leads us to the heart of every culture, with all of its history, values, and challenges, and bids us to live and to speak. To ignore sociopolitical issues is not to follow Jesus to the cross, where the leading Romans and Jews await, but to sneak away from Gethsemane by night. It is to pray half of Jesus' prayer in Gethsemane: "Father, let this cup pass from me"—and not to finish with "But not my will but yours be done" (Mark 14:36).

We've all seen the ugliness of a church withdrawing from public life—with all of its sociopolitical challenges—and awaiting the day when Jesus will return to rescue them from the wicked world and all of its problems.

We've also seen the ugliness of a church whose entire vision of reality is wholly contained within and enslaved to a particular political party to which they've prostituted themselves.

We can afford to do neither.

We must not collude with Caiaphas or Pilate.

Nor can we simply stay in Gethsemane.

We've got to make that lonely walk to Golgotha, right through the midst of Caiaphas and Pilate, drawing the brokenness of the world onto ourselves as we carry that suprapolitical banner: "Jesus of Nazareth, King of the Jews."

Becoming Human[1]

For Ben, the Christosist.

MOST WESTERN CHRISTIANS' CONCEPTION of personal "ethics" or "sanctification"—that is, of the present progress and future goal of our "moral lives"—isn't especially Christian but owes, rather, to some very particular strands of philosophical thought in Western history.

Since the beginning of Christian history—and reaching potent expression in various monastic movements—some Christians have succumbed to a thoroughgoing "asceticism": that is, to various kinds of "world denial" and "self-denial."

It can all appear very "Christian," of course, very biblical on the surface of it. After all, the Bible teaches us that we're a mess after Genesis 3. Let's take Paul, for instance. He tells us that "all sinned and have fallen short of the glory of God" (Rom 3:23), that "no one is right with God" (Rom 3:10), and that, indeed, our only hope of a glorious future is through the death of our old selves and the resurrection of our new selves through baptism into the Messiah Jesus (Rom 6:1–11).

So, it's settled, right?

---

1. For some of the thoughts reflected in this chapter, see Wright, *After You Believe.*

Well, not quite.

After all, some of the ascetical tendencies that crept into earliest Christianity—and which had, actually, already found a home in certain strands of pre-Christian Judaism—owed much of their initial impetus to a kind of Platonic dualism. To be clear, ascetical tendencies were characteristic of many ancient religious traditions and are characteristic of many modern ones as well. But there is little doubt that it is specifically Platonic dualism which has exercised the most influence on ascetical Christian traditions.

And for the Platonic tradition, materiality, with all of its needs (food, water, etc.), challenges (change, atrophy), and passions and pleasures (food, alcohol, sex, aesthetics), is a lower and less desirable state of existence than immateriality. So, on this worldview, the world as such, materiality as such, and our embodied experience as such, are to be outright denied and transcended.

Hence, some monastic Christian traditions have looked as though they weren't only after the denial of our *sinful corruption*, of the world's *sinful corruption*, but of our embodied, material existence and location as such. Quiet solitude can be good, both geographically (in a monastery) and relationally (e.g., celibacy). But there's a grave danger, at least from the Christian perspective, in rejecting our entire embodied experience and the material world in which we live.

After all, from the Christian perspective, unlike the Platonic, the creation is, however presently broken and marred, ultimately good and headed for resurrection. And physical human beings are, however broken, corrupted, and presently decaying, headed for bodily resurrection.

The Platonic tendencies, then, amount to a rejection of Genesis 1–2: the created world is a not a good gift of the creator God that will continue and grow under the gentle stewardship of God's human creatures.

The Christian response to Platonic dualism is this: the created world, and embodied human beings within it, are indeed corrupted, but the answer is not to escape materiality once and for all but to rescue this material universe from its corruption and to continue the project of Genesis 1–2.

Genesis 3 does not erase Genesis 1–2.

Okay, so much for Platonic dualism.

We now jump to the post-Enlightenment influences of "Romanticism" and "Existentialism."

Romanticism emphasized, among other things, impulsivity and spontaneity over the moral disciplines of discernment and occasional denial—the latter of which, so Romanticism has often insisted, always and necessarily involves an unhealthy suppression and/or rejection of your "true self." Hereby Romanticism anticipated—or perhaps partly gave birth to—some of the tendencies of postmodernism.

Existentialism insisted that what mattered most was one's own deep, internal, experiential "sense" of the truth, certainly not what "institutional Christianity" had to say and still less the stultifying Christian "disciplines" that were said to produce holiness and genuine humanness.

When we also take into account the strong undercurrent of philosophical idealism, issuing not least from Rene Descartes's (eighteenth-century) radical skepticism and insisting upon the primacy of the mind's inner states over our embodied experience of and within the material universe, we're starting to come close to our present situation.

This is the complex world in which we must live and to which we must speak.

We must say, over against certain kinds of radical asceticism: "The earth"—however presently broken and corrupted—"is the LORD's and all that is in it" (Ps 24:1 NRSV). We must say, over against Romantic, Existentialist postmodernism: "some things truly are evil and destructive, and they must be outright denied and not simply redefined."

So, to ask the question in a different way: Are we supposed to deny ourselves and this world or are we supposed to drink it in? Are we supposed to be characterized by suffering or by celebration and victory?

The answer is . . .

Both.

But why?

Because of the story. The world is a corrupt and broken place. Not all of it without discrimination is to be celebrated and enjoyed. Much of it stands against the good purposes of God and the ultimate flourishing of the world. Much of it is utterly destructive. This is the bit which, if you're going to flourish, you have to "deny" with zeal.

However, and this has always been the danger with certain ascetical tendencies, you have to make sure that your posture of denial doesn't go beyond the serious recognition of Genesis 3 to a rejection of Genesis 1–2. God's world, though broken and corrupted, retains its intrinsic goodness *and will be rescued.*

Okay, so much for all of that.

But what about the nature of our "moral lives" in relation to all of this?

More particularly, how we are to understand the relationship between divine and human agency in this connection, the relationship between God's activity and our activity?

The key to this all-important question, I suggest, is the logic of Genesis 1:26–28, and of the way in which this text was read in earliest Christianity.

"Then God said, 'Let *us* make humankind in our image, according to our likeness . . .'" (Gen 1:26 NRSV).

What's the "*us*" about?

According to Paul and the early Christians, God the Father is here talking to God the Son, *in whose image and likeness human beings are made.* Or, to use Paul's language from Romans 8:29: "Those whom he foreknew, he also predestined to share the same form as *the image of his son . . .*"

But what does this mean?

To get the point we've got to see the forward thrust of what Paul's saying. He's *not* conceiving of a static picture in which, in the beginning, God created Adam and Eve according to the pattern of the (at that time) preincarnate Son and that at the very moment of their creation they were already all that God intended them to be.

No. Paul's vision of creation isn't static.

What Paul's saying, rather, is that in the beginning the Father, by the Spirit, created human beings according to the image/pattern of the preincarnate Son, *but toward the goal of them growing up into the fullness of the Son who would become incarnate, die, rise, and be glorified.*

When Adam and Eve were created, they were "perfect" in the sense that they were made by a perfect God and were without sin.

But they were not yet all that they would be.

They were created in hope. They were created to *become*, to mature, to grow into the fullness of the Son who would become incarnate, live, die, rise, and be glorified.

God created humans in the hope that they would one day participate by the spirit in a relationship with the father patterned precisely after the father's unique relationship with the son.

But wait.

Isn't the Son intrinsic to God, the Second Person of the Trinity?

Indeed.

So, from this angle, we can see that God's plan was something like this: to create creatures other than himself who would one day, by the spirit, be patterned after his own Son and so included within his own divine, trinitarian life.

And here's the point: in the logic of Genesis 1:26–28 and of the way in which this text was read in early Christianity, *to become more truly human is to participate more and more in God's own divine life.*

But what does any of this have to do with ethics, with sanctification, with the means and mechanism of our behavior?

This is the point: the above Christian vision, based upon the early Christian reading of Genesis 1:26–28, immediately and ultimately renders most would-be Christian visions of "ethics," and of the relationship between divine and human agency, problematic.

After all, most would-be Christian visions of "ethics" have at their heart the notion that humanity's fundamental posture toward God is one of "obedience." God and his agency stand over against us and our agency and we are to "obey" him. But does the logic of the early Christian reading of Genesis 1:26–28 encourage us to think in this way?

After all, "obedience" only has a proper place in the context of ignorance and/or sin. We must obey God because he sees and knows what we do not see and know. Or, we must obey God because his will for us is good while our wills for ourselves and for others are at times destructive.

But imagine the future; imagine God's new world. We won't be, according to Christian tradition, susceptible to sin. Nor will ignorance, it seems, *fundamentally* characterize our existence. That's not to say, of course, that humans will be omniscient; it's just to say that ignorance will not characterize our existence as it does now (so 1 Cor 13:8–13). But, if, as we've just considered, "obedience" only has its proper place within the context of ignorance and/or sinfulness, then it stands to reason that "obedience" is not, cannot, and will not be our ultimate posture toward God.

Of course, we do well now to remember that we are often bedeviled by both ignorance and sinfulness. But we also do well to remember that Christians should always be aiming for God's new world, and in that new world we will be so filled with the Third Person of the Trinity as to be in desire and in will indistinguishable from the now-incarnate Second Person of the Trinity.

In this connection, we tend to think of divine agency and human agency in fundamentally competitive, "zero-sum" terms. *Either* God does this or that *or* we do this or that, but the "agency" in question is conceived in competitive terms.

It's *either* God's grace *or* it's our works.

It's *either* predestination *or* it's free will.

But we have to let the early Christian reading of Genesis 1:26–28 challenge these (false) antitheses.

God's will and agency are always in accordance with what is good, what is right, and what is true.[2] Our wills and agencies waver this way and that either because we don't know what is good, right, and true, or because we don't have the moral capacity to bring it about. However, if what is good, right, and true is always for our good, and if we knew how to determine what was good, right, and true and had the capacity to bring it about, then we would *always* do what is good, right, and true.

---

2. Of course, and understandably, some would rather put it this way: certain things are good and right and true *because they are in accordance with God's nature.*

And this is precisely what the Christian faith promises us by the Spirit. Humans presently enslaved to their own moral ignorance and impotence will be fully set free both to see and to do the good.

In this regard, therefore, human agency will always and necessarily agree with the will of God, being set free from ignorance and sin. But this won't mean that humans aren't "free" and/or that God's will and agency have erased ours, but that humans enslaved to ignorance and sin will finally be free *for the first time* ever to see and to do the good.

And this ought to color everything we think about a Christian vision of "ethics." It's not primarily about "obedience," as though the goal were for our ignorant and/or sinful agencies ever to obey someone or something else. Christian "ethics" is not fundamentally about "saying no" to ourselves, at least not in any ultimate sense, though at the moment it will necessarily involve that.

Christian "ethics" is about becoming human in the Genesis 1:26–28 sense.

If God had wanted mindless puppets of slavish obedience, then that's what he would have created.

Instead, God wants truly free agents who do what is Christlike because they're fully free and mature to see it and to do it.

In this regard, many people wrongly assume that, at present, they're "free" and that the Christian faith promises a kind of "slavery" or total rejection of their own "agency/freedom." However, exactly the opposite is the case. It's rather that a rejection of participating in God's divine life, a grasping after a freedom apart from participation in God, produces a shrunken humanness enslaved to the very few predictable options of self-gratification.

However, on the other hand, a deep participation in God's own divine life—the only place where true freedom exists—liberates us from ourselves and from our own grasping sense of freedom apart from God wherein we, for the first time and increasingly, discover new heights and depths and breadths of freedom. What we actually discover is that there's more possibility for human creativity, choice, and freedom *within the holy and divine life of God* than ever could be attained in the necessarily shrunken and increasingly shrinking world that exists apart from the creative and sustaining life of God.

CONSTRUCTIVE PROPOSALS

The previous section of this book was largely stage-setting, as much deconstructive as constructive. The following section is more straightforwardly constructive in terms of offering fresh proposals about key areas of Christian theology and life.

Scripture:
Tricky Texts and Issues

I HAVE, OF COURSE, already said plenty about Scripture, but so much of what I've said has been by way of deconstruction; or, on the other hand, so much of what I've said has been about the massive storyline of Scripture. In that sense, I've been concerned with how we should treat the Bible at a macro-level. But what about individual parts of the Bible, or, indeed, individual challenges of interpretation therein?

For instance, e.g., (1) what about Genesis 1–2 and modern science; (2) Genesis 6–9 and God's mercy and patience; and (3) the Israelite conquest and God's universal love? Let's take these issues in turn.

GENESIS 1–2 AND MODERN SCIENCE

At a macro-level, "evolution" is less of a "theory" and more of an established fact of science beyond reasonable doubt, though, of course, there are plenty of debates to be had about how exactly things began, developed, and under what circumstances, etc. But that the material universe began roughly fourteen billion years ago and has evolved— as have all living organisms within it—into the universe in which we are now living seems to be a fact of science (beyond reasonable doubt) as established as, for example, heliocentrism (that the earth revolves around the sun rather than the other way around).

In terms of the observable evidence, therefore, "Young Earthism"—i.e., the view that the universe began (as a literalistic reading of Genesis would have it) less than 10,000 years ago—appears to be special pleading, ultimately forcing folks to say something like: "Well, indeed, the universe *appears* to be billions of years old, in terms of the scientifically observable evidence, but that doesn't mean that it actually *is* billions of years old. Perhaps, in order to confound our rationality, to teach us not to rely upon the fragility of human reason, God made the universe to have the *appearance* of billions of years of age when, in actuality, he created it just several thousand years ago."

But this isn't very convincing, and, in particular, it struggles to make sense of Genesis 1:26–28 (and of so much else in the Bible). Genesis 1:26–28 tells us that God fashioned humans according to his "image" and "likeness" and in such a way that, furthermore, "human ways of knowing" (including "reason" and "scientific knowledge" dependent upon the operations of "reason") are not objectionable from God's perspective but are, rather, part of what it means to be made in God's image and likeness.

The modern, theological rejection of human reason owes particularly to Martin Luther's misreading of Paul's theology.[1] For Luther, Paul, the greatest and most prolific early Christian theologian, had fundamentally opposed God's agency to human agency, God's grace to human works, God's omniscience to the futility of human knowledge, etc.[2] But it is demonstrable—and, indeed, it has been demonstrated—that this is not the thrust of Paul's theology. In any case, that's for another time. For now, I simply note that this antirational theology is not biblical: it neither corresponds to the biblical view of humans as creatures made in God's image and likeness, nor does it correspond to Paul's understanding of the relationship between divine and human agency.

1. This doesn't mean, of course, that there aren't great strengths in Luther's theological program.

2. Of course, one could trace this dynamic back to Augustine and probably further.

Of course, for the Bible, sin corrupts everything in God's creation, including human knowing, but human ways of knowing *per se* are not fundamentally objectionable in the Bible.

But, to return to the point: What does all of this have to do with Genesis 1–2 and evolution? Well, in Genesis, not only is the earth presented as very, very young in terms of the findings of modern science, but, to take one prominent feature of the text, all of the creatures in the universe are created "directly" by God—i.e., it is not imagined that some evolved from others.

Of course, one of the most controversial points is that, in Genesis, humans are created *ex nihilo* (as a new and fresh act of God) and do not evolve from earlier primates. What are we to do with this? Are we to say that the vast majority (virtually all) of evolutionary biologists are unwittingly incorrect or that they're part of some large-scale scam, even though such evolutionary biologists span generations, geographical locales, institutions, and economic, social, and political agendas? It strains credulity to believe that the whole thing is a hoax, not to mention that some of the (admittedly highly technical) evidence is increasingly available for a popular audience.

No.

We have to do business with evolutionary science. That's the way it is. And, in any case, when you look at the rich Jewish and Christian history of reading the early parts of Genesis, many readers have rightly realized that we're not dealing here with "history" and much less with a primitive, scientific account of biological origins. That's simply not the genre of Genesis 1–11.

Genesis 1–2, then—so far from attempting to offer a literalistic, scientific account of biological origins—is telling *the theological truth about the universe.*

That is, Genesis 1–2 (and 1–11 as a whole) is more interested in these questions: (1) who is God; (2) what is God like; (3) what's the universe like, particularly in theological terms; (4) is the universe *ultimately* disordered, chaotic, dangerous, and pointless, or does it have a structure, a beauty, and an intended goal; (5) what's the point of animal life; (6) what is the role and function of human beings within this whole thing; and (7) how do humans relate to God?

If the writer essentially answers these questions—and there are others—then he's going to be pretty happy with what he's written. How, in modern, scientific terms, "it all came about," is less important to him.

It is, therefore, a category mistake to frame the question like this: "Can Genesis 1–2 *and* evolutionary science be true?"

The answer is: "Of course."

But they are "true" in different ways.

One is an experimental assessment of materiality and its history.

One is an account of "the meaning of life."

They're both true, but in different senses.

However many challenges this creates for Christian theology, however many loose ends, however many adjustments, however many fresh and creative angles of vision, it's where we have to go.

GENESIS 6–9 AND GOD'S MERCY AND PATIENCE

We now come to a particularly challenging passage: by Genesis 6, still very early in the story, God is already overwhelmed by human wickedness. He is so overwhelmed, in fact, that he decides to purge the world of human beings and to start over. That is the context of Noah, his ark, and the famous flood.

The story tells us that God preserved Noah, his family, and a representative number of the animals. But the rest of the world— men, women, children, and the rest of the animals—were drowned in the flood.

So we come to a very difficult question: Does this story appear to reveal the same God as the one we meet in Jesus?

The answer is "Yes" and "No"—*but*, before anyone cries "Heresy," let me provide the crucial clarifications.

As to the "No": the Gospels give us a rather robust portrait of Jesus of Nazareth, in whom, so all four Gospels and the rest of the New Testament tell us, God is fully and decisively unveiled. And

Jesus' character is clear and consistent. In particular, when Jesus is crucified, during his moment of deepest pain and abandonment, he utters these words: "Father, forgive them; for they do not know what they are doing" (Luke 23:34 NRSV).

This text, coming from the lips of God incarnate, cannot be inconsequential to the way in which we think about God's judgment, either in the present or in the ultimate future.

So, as to the "No," I simply do not think that this Jesus, this God incarnate, would have "sent" the flood described in Genesis 6–9. To say that he would, I fear, would run the risk of ascribing to God the equivalent of a "split personality."

But what about the "Yes?" When the genre of Genesis 1–11 is appreciated, and when the nature of the flood story within that genre is appreciated, *the character of an immensely good and gracious God emerges bright and clear.*

In terms of its genre, Genesis 1–11 is "myth," which is to say that it's less interested in literalistic biological and historical details and more interested in expounding a distinctly Jewish (and biblical) view of the meaning of life, of the nature of God, of creation, of humans, etc.

But here's the thing: before the writing of Genesis 1–11, other cultures had already tried their hand at expounding a foundational myth. Indeed, numerous societies had even told similar flood stories. But perhaps of most relevance to Genesis 6–9 is the ancient Akkadian myth (in its Old Babylonian form, ~1700 BCE) of Atrahasis, a myth in which, when the gods had attempted (once again!) to destroy all of humanity (this time by a flood), Atrahasis built a boat big enough for himself, his family, and his livestock. As such, he was able to survive the deluge. Horrifyingly, however, we later discover that the reason for the deluge in the first place was simply divine "population control."

This myth was widely disseminated and well-known. It contained perhaps the most popular flood story of the ancient world. So, when we locate Genesis 6–9 within its ancient context—that is, within the proper context of its divine "inspiration"—in relation to Atrahasis and similar stories, a few things become clear:

1. The writer of Genesis 6–9 is not creating the idea of a divine flood from nothing. Rather, that was a given of his ancient context. No one doubted it. It would have been nonsensical to think otherwise. The story of the world involved a massive, divinely authorized flood. That was all there was to it. You couldn't deny it; all you could do was interpret it.

2. So, when the writer of Genesis 6–9 tells us a flood story, it's not so much that he's writing theology "from scratch." He is, rather, *entering into an ancient, standard theological conversation on its own terms, offering his own creative interpretation.*

3. The universe isn't, so the writer is saying, an ultimately dark, incoherent, immoral place of self-interested divine combat. And, as such, the flood couldn't have been the result of disputes among the gods about how best to have more leisure and/or to control the human population—after all, in *this* story, the true God made humans in his image and likeness and to be "fruitful and multiply" (Gen 1).

4. Rather, "If we *must* tell a flood story," the writer thinks, "we'll tell it like this. There's an incomparably good God who made and loves the world and who wants to see its flourishing and not its corruption and destruction. Thus, this good God sent purgative waters to wash away the world's corruption and injustice and thus to restart the project he'd begun in Genesis 1–2: to "flood" the world with his own justice and peace in and through creatures made in his image and likeness."

That, I think, is how the flood story works. To make it a theological statement of "first principles"—as though the writer were simply beginning from scratch and attempting to tell his audience "what God is like"—would be a mistake.

THE CONQUEST AND GOD'S UNIVERSAL LOVE

We now come to another tricky issue: what are we to make of the whole narrative—from Joshua through Judges in particular—of "the Israelite Conquest," in which the Old Testament recounts that God himself had instructed the Israelites to enter into the promised land of Canaan and to eradicate it of all of its pagan peoples: men, women, and children?

I especially note this point in this connection: in the book of Joshua, it is the Jewish leader and successor of Moses, *Yehoshua* ("Joshua"), who leads Israel on its violent, military conquest of the promised land, whereas in the New Testament it is a very different kind of *Yeshua/Yehoshua* (Jesus' name in his native Aramaic) who leads a very different kind of (nonviolent) conquest. I highly doubt this point was missed by Jesus and his earliest followers.

So, *at the theological level*, what are we to make of the Conquest Narrative? Is it a full and true revelation of the God we meet in Christ? It seems to me here that we must say "No." The God we meet in Christ simply would not have gone about things like this.

So what does that mean? Should we, like the second-century heretic, Marcion, reject the Old Testament?

By no means!—but we *must* learn to read it like Jesus and the earliest Christians.

Jesus and the earliest Christians treated the Old Testament as a massive narrative *leading up* to Jesus, his mission, and his message. And, in this way, they *did not* treat the Old Testament—irrespective of its reception and interpretation in earliest Christianity—as a full and final revelation of the true God.

Rather, they treated the Old Testament as a fully inspired narrative whose proper meaning and interpretation could only be attained *retrospectively*, in Christ and by the Spirit.

Jesus was and is the full and decisive revelation of the nature and character of the true God—everything leading up to him was partial and progressive revelation.

Most Christians know this instinctively, but the point still needs to be made.

This is, after all, the way Jesus saw things.

Let's take a famous example.

In Deuteronomy 24:1–4, it is clear that Moses, here speaking for God, allowed an Israelite male to discard his wife by divorce if "she does not please him because he finds something objectionable about her" (v. 1 NRSV). Now, in the ancient context within which Deuteronomy was written, the ethics of the divorce laws fare pretty well when compared with the practices of other ancient societies; but this is *not* Jesus' view, even though it's in Deuteronomy and even though it was, therefore, naturally accepted by other leading Jews:

> Some Pharisees came, and to test him they asked, 'Is it lawful for a man to divorce his wife?' He answered them, 'What did Moses command you?' They said, 'Moses allowed a man to write a certificate of dismissal and to divorce her.' But Jesus said to them, 'He wrote this commandment for you because of the hardness of your heart.' (Mark 10:2–5 NRSV)

Because of the hardness of your heart.

In other words, that's not *really* what God wanted to say, but you weren't prepared to hear what God wanted to say.

In other words, though the Old Testament is the inspired *narrative* that leads up to and contextualizes Jesus, early Christianity, and the whole New Testament, and though it is the inspired, *progressive* revelation of God, it is, *according to Jesus himself*, not the full and final word on the true God.

That word belongs to, and simply *is*, Jesus himself, whether people are prepared to hear it or not.

For Jesus, as for the earliest Christians, the Old Testament only takes on its proper significance when it's seen as an inspired narrative that reaches a climax in the life, death, and resurrection of Jesus, from which vantage point alone it can be seen and read Christianly.

Atonement[1]

For Paul, a relentless exegete

WE NOW COME TO one of the most central questions of Christian theology, a question which has implications for our view of "who God is," "who/what humans are," "the nature of evil and sin," and "judgment" and "salvation." This is the question: What happened on the cross?

What did God "accomplish?"

What does the cross say about God?

About Jesus?

About humans?

About sin?

About judgment?

About salvation?

There are, of course, long-held and well-known views, represented both in the ancient and in the modern church:

1. *Christus Victor*
2. Penal Substitution
3. Satisfaction
4. Moral Example

1. On atonement, see also Wright, *Day the Revolution Began.*

There are others, as well as nuances of opinion within the views listed above. But the above sampling of major views is enough to make the points I want to make in what follows.

For some Christians, both ancient and modern, what is *really* happening in the atonement—in the crucifixion of Jesus and, of course, in the resurrection and ascension as well—is that God in Christ is defeating the dark, suprahuman forces of evil in the world and thereby establishing his gracious sovereignty over that world. In other words, the cross is the place and moment at which God in Christ has a great *victory* over the dark forces of evil.

Concomitantly, the cross is *not* the place, for many who hold the *Christus Victor* view, where God pours out his wrath. It is not the place, in other words, where the sins of the world are *condemned* in the sinless Christ (so Penal Substitution). Nor is the cross the place where God, whose perfect holiness and righteousness necessarily demand punitive judgment upon sin and an exaction for the human failure properly to ascribe to him glory, "satisfies" (so Satisfaction) his own proper desire for glory. And though, furthermore, Jesus' sacrificial death can and does serve as an example of self-giving love to be imitated, its moral-exemplary function (so Moral Example) is not primary.

Rather, for the *Christus Victor* view, what principally matters is that, since Genesis 3, the universe (and humans beings within it) has been dominated by dark, suprahuman forces of evil; and in the cross—along with the resurrection and ascension—God in Christ has conquered these forces and taken from them the cosmic sovereignty which they've (in a sense) enjoyed since the fall.

This view, I think, has a lot going for it. First of all, it seems to have been a major feature of Jesus' own understanding of the atonement. We can see the point in the so-called "Temptation Narrative" (Matt 4:1–11; Mark 1:12–13; Luke 4:1–13). Jesus has just been anointed by the Spirit for his unique and decisive messianic vocation (Matt 3:13–17; Mark 2:9–11; Luke 3:21–22), in which he will embody and enact God's rescue of Israel and the world. Astonishingly, however, and immediately following this anointing, Jesus is "cast" by the Spirit (Mark 1:12) out into the wilderness so that he can be tested by "Satan."

Now, don't get hung up on this last point.

Some will say: "See, you lost me right there. I just can't believe in that sort of thing—a lead demonic figure dressed in red tights and carrying a pitchfork."

Again, don't misunderstand the nature of ancient Jewish apocalyptic and thereby miss the point.

The point of ancient Jewish reflection on "demons" and "the devil" is really to say this:

· 1. There is evil in the world.

2. And it seems as though the nature, extent, and force of evil cannot be wholly accounted for by calculating the sum-total of sinful human inclinations and actions.

3. Thus, there seems to be an even darker, suprahuman force and energy in the world which is opposed to the good purposes of God.

4. And it is this force(s), crucially, which is the root problem with which God must deal if he hopes fully to establish his kingdom on earth as it is in heaven.

Okay—back to the point. The Gospels tell the story of Jesus in such a way that the anointing leads straight to the "Temptation Narrative," so that the reader sees that Jesus' principal enemy and challenge is actually not the pagan empire of Rome, nor the general sinfulness of human beings, but, rather, the much darker and more mysterious suprahuman forces of evil.

This theme, too, is the point of the exorcisms (for example, Mark 1:21–28; 5:1–20). Jesus isn't just performing random, dramatic miracles for their own sake. Rather, he is establishing his good kingdom *precisely by overthrowing the forces of evil*. Nor is this theme confined to the early parts of the gospel narrative. Rather, it goes right to the end. Luke 22:3 vividly makes the point. Judas has agreed to betray Jesus—which will, of course, precipitate the events which lead to the crucifixion—and Luke tells us: "Then Satan entered into Judas called Iscariot . . . So he consented and began to look for an opportunity to betray him" (Luke 22:3–6 NRSV).

So "demonic" activity bookends Jesus' ministry. His whole life and ministry is a battle with the dark forces of evil. Jesus knew that and embraced it. The cross—and, following it, the resurrection and ascension—would be the means by which he would wrestle cosmic sovereignty from the dark forces of evil and thereby establish his kingdom.

As I said, therefore, the *Christus Victor* view has a lot going for it. But this is the question: Should we emphasize the *Christus Victor* model of the atonement *to the total exclusion of the other views?* I think not, particularly in relation to Penal Substitution.

I do think that we can say, however, that the satisfaction theory has little going for it. The idea that the God of the Bible requires some kind of arbitrary exaction for offenses committed against his holiness and righteousness and for a failure to properly ascribe to him glory is not very convincing on biblical grounds. That view of God's character just doesn't emerge from the biblical narrative.

The moral example view, on the other hand, while not totally wrong-headed, is clearly insufficient in itself. While it is true that Jesus' self-giving unto death served as a model of love, sacrifice, and others-centeredness for the early Christians (see, for example, Phil 2:5–11), this is not the primary meaning of the cross.

After all, taken by itself, this would imply that the principal problem with the world and with human beings was simply that we didn't have a proper example. In this case, there would be nothing deeper, nothing more fundamentally wrong. Whereas, for Jesus and the earliest Christians, something was profoundly wrong with human beings and with the whole universe. What was required was not simply a helpful moral example but a divine act of transformative significance whereby (1) the forces of evil were defeated; (2) sin was condemned; (3) and the consequent possibility of a brand new humanness was introduced by the outpouring of the Spirit.

In relation to point (2) above, we now consider the Penal Substitution view. Without elements of this view, any account of the atonement is incomplete. Particularly relevant is one central, sacramental biblical tradition and one Pauline text, and both in relation to the crucifixion itself. Of course, the topic deserves a thorough treatment of dozens and dozens of texts and traditions, and not least Isaiah 53, Zechariah 9–14, Daniel 7–9, several psalms, many noncanonical texts from the period, and, of course, countless New

Testament passages. But we're attempting a "brief sketch," though one that is still representative of Scripture as a whole.

Let's take the Lord's Supper first. In all four Gospels, Jesus makes his final, fateful trip to the holy city at Passover, one of the seven major Jewish festivals. Passover commemorates the time when God rescued the Israelites from Egypt and led them through the Red Sea. Recall that God had heard the cries of his enslaved people (Exod 2:23; 3:7, 9) and had commissioned Moses to announce to Pharaoh, the king of Egypt: "Thus says the Lord: 'Israel is my firstborn son. I said to you, "Let my son go that he may worship me." But you refused to let him go; now I will kill your firstborn son'" (Exod 4:21–23).

The first Passover had involved the death of Egyptian first-borns. The new Passover would involve the death of God's firstborn.

But here's the catch. After the Exodus, the gift of Torah at Mount Sinai, the wilderness wanderings, the entering into the promised land, and the Davidic and Solomonic kingdoms, Israel committed large-scale idolatry, as the history writers of 1–2 Samuel, 1–2 Kings, 1–2 Chronicles, and prophet after prophet tell us. Israel had broken the covenant and gone into Babylonian exile for her sins.

> The LORD, the God of their ancestors, sent persistently to them by his messengers, because he had compassion on his people and on his dwelling place; but they kept mocking the messengers of God, despising his words, and scoffing at his prophets, until the wrath of the LORD against his people became so great that there was no remedy. Therefore he brought up against them the king of the Chaldeans, who killed their youths with the sword in the house of their sanctuary, and had no compassion on young man or young woman, the aged or the feeble; he gave them all into his hand. (2 Chr 36:15–17 NRSV)

As devastating as this state of affairs was, Jeremiah the prophet—not unlike Isaiah and some of the other prophets—held out the wonderful hope of a new exodus, but this time it would be out of Egypt, not Babylon:

> Therefore, the days are surely coming, says the LORD, when it shall no longer be said, "As the LORD lives who brought the people of Israel up out of the land of Egypt," but "As the LORD lives who brought the people of Israel up out of the land of the north and out of all the lands where he had driven them." For I will bring them back to their own land that I gave to their ancestors. (Jer 16:14–15 NRSV)

Essentially, Jeremiah records God as saying: "Remember how I conquered a pagan nation and rescued you the first time? I can do it again!"

But there's one crucial difference. The first exodus had nothing to do with the "forgiveness of sins." Israel hadn't been "sent" into Egyptian slavery because she'd committed grave sins like idolatry. On the other hand, however, Israel *had* been sent into Babylonian exile because of her idolatry.

So, insofar as the prophets had appropriated the theme of a new exodus, they had done so with a crucial twist: this new exodus, this new "redemption" from slavery would be the sign that God had forgiven Israel's sins:

> Comfort, O comfort my people,
>   says your God.
> Speak tenderly to Jerusalem,
>   and cry to her
> that she has served her term,
>   that her penalty is paid,
> that she has received from the LORD's hand
>   double for all her sins. (Isa 40:1–2 NRSV)

And it seems to be, among other things, this new-exodus-as-forgiveness-of-sins that John the Baptist was picking up when he decided to baptize Israelites in the Jordan River "for the forgiveness of [their] sins" (Mark 1:4). The decision to perform this great prophetic enactment of a new exodus and thus a new entry into the promised land—which is what the baptism of John was all about—set the stage for the entirety of Jesus' ministry.

Moreover, when we come near to the end of Jesus' ministry, we see that the new-exodus-as-forgiveness-of-sins bookends the life of Jesus. Jesus had quite deliberately decided to begin with John's baptism; and so he had also quite deliberately decided to go that last fateful time to Jerusalem at the time of Passover, the great celebration of the first exodus.

And not long before his night-time arrest, Jesus decided to hold the Passover celebration with his disciples but with an even more shocking twist. Neither the Gospels nor Paul (Matt 26:26–29; Mark 14:22–25; Luke 22:14–23; and 1 Cor 11:23–26) tell us that Jesus or his disciples had procured and/or sacrificed (i.e., slaughtered) a paschal lamb for their dinner celebration. This would, however, have been the center of the celebration for most ancient Jews.

But bread and wine they had, and, so Jesus would intimate, a paschal lamb all the same:

> While they were eating, he took a loaf of bread, and after blessing it he broke it, gave it to them, and said, "Take; this is my body." Then he took a cup, and after giving thanks he gave it to them, and all of them drank from it. He said to them, "This is my blood of the covenant, which is poured out for many." (Mark 14:22–24 NRSV)

It's an exodus meal, a celebration. But there's no slaughtered lamb, just Jesus himself offering bread-as-his-body in view of his coming death. Likewise the cup. This time it would be neither the Egyptians' nor the Israelites'; God himself, rather, would lose his own Son, and his blood would be wiped across the doorpost of the universe.[2]

The reference to "my blood of the covenant" is taken from Exodus 24:8, where it refers to the blood by which Israel was bound to YHWH in the first covenant at Mount Sinai. But now, on the lips of Jesus, it refers to the blood of the new covenant (so Luke 22:20) that is the sign and symbol of the new exodus, Jesus' own blood that is "poured out for many" (Mark 14:24).

Okay, so a few crucial things have become clear:

---

2. I've taken the delightful phrase "blood on the doorpost(s) of the universe" from Bell and Golden, *Jesus Wants to Save Christians*, ch. 6.

1. Jesus, picking up the theme of a new-exodus-as-forgiveness-of-sins, construed his entire ministry as the enactment of the new exodus.
2. But this new exodus, unlike the first one, would not be just for Israel's rescue from slavery but for the great reckoning of Israel and the worlds' sins.
3. Indeed, this time God's firstborn, the Passover lamb, would be "poured out for many."

But where is "God" in all this?

That is one of the central questions atonement theology must answer. Is Jesus divine or isn't he? And if he's divine, and if the context of his divinity is first-century Jewish monotheism, then how does Jesus-as-divine relate to the one whom he regularly called "Father" (not to mention the Holy Spirit at this point)? And, particularly, how do our answers to these questions relate to what's happening on the cross?

If Jesus isn't properly divine—if he isn't "intrinsic" to the single divine reality at the heart of the universe (so trinitarian theology)—then God is effectively dealing with sin *outside* of himself and in another "person/place."

Or if Jesus somehow *ceases* to be properly divine by the time of the crucifixion, then, again, the divine reality (God) is "punishing" sin *somewhere else, in someone else.*

And, indeed, many Christians think about Jesus and the cross in this way.

And this is, furthermore, why so many Christians have such an awkward relationship with Easter—and, indeed, why so many Christians love "Jesus" but don't know how to feel about God "the father." It's not hard to see. In this schema, *Jesus* suffers on our behalf but God the father is somewhere else, inflicting *and not absorbing* the punishment.

But this is a mistake.

All four Gospels and the rest of the New Testament, not to mention the subsequent Christian tradition, is clear: Jesus is the embodiment of the Second Person of the triune God, the Son of the Father in the Spirit. What Jesus experiences, the one God experiences; what the son experiences, the other two persons of the Trinity experience.

But now we come to the opposite mistake.

A great many Christians, reacting to the above schema of a nondivine Jesus suffering at the hands of the father, have gone the other way and said that Jesus, and particularly when he suffers on the cross, embodies the reality of the one God in totality, without any sense of a trinitarian dynamic. But what does that mean, and what is gained by this way of looking at it?

What is gained is that you no longer have "God" *somewhere else, punishing someone else.* Rather, in this schema God is just as subject to the power, force, and consequences of sin as anyone else: indeed, he suffers under its force.

But is that actually the way forward?

Does this schema properly capture *both* biblical emphases: that (1) the true God takes the full force of sin upon himself in the crucifixion of Jesus; and that, (2) in the crucifixion of Jesus, the true God pronounces his decisive judgment upon sin, his great and decisive "No" to all that corrupts his beautiful creation?

To take both emphases with equal seriousness, we have to say something like the following: (1) Jesus remains fully God, the Second Person of the Trinity, at and during the crucifixion; and (2) the one God "condemns" sin in the person of Jesus. For this latter point, we turn to a key text from Paul's letter to the Romans (8:3): "For what the Torah could not do—because of the incapacity of the corrupt human condition—God has done: having sent his own son in the likeness of sinful flesh and as a sin offering, he condemned sin in his [Jesus'] flesh."

Now to unpack this incredibly dense text.

Leaving aside for the moment the bit about the Torah, we consider what God has done in Jesus.

Note: in Jesus, and particularly in his crucifixion, God condemns *sin* and *not* Jesus.

You see, for a great many people, in the way in which they think about penal substitution, a "penalty" for sin hung over human beings, and Jesus, our "substitute," took that penalty upon himself and was thereby condemned. So, in this schema, God had planned to condemn *human beings*.

Strictly speaking, that's wrong.

The God who loves the world and who can always make the distinction between its glory and its corruption had intended in Jesus *to condemn the corruption of the world* and not his glorious creatures.

And here we see how penal substitution joins up with *Christus Victor*.

For Jesus, Paul, and the early Christians, the *ultimate* enemy is not sinful human beings but, rather, the dark, suprahuman, anti-God forces in the world that, in Genesis 3, are symbolized by the snake.

And note: the snake's rebellion clearly precedes and partly generates the rebellion of human beings.

So, in the crucifixion, God's purpose was to deal finally, once and for all, with these dark forces, forces which, through their own deceit and through human idolatry, had become deeply entangled with God's good human creatures.

So the good God, in a great act of substitutionary condemnation (Penal Substitution), drew the dark forces of evil and all human sin upon his very self in the incarnate, Second Person of the Trinity, the crucified Jesus of Nazareth. And this great act of penal substitution is precisely the means by which God in Christ has the great victory over all the forces of evil (*Christus Victor*).

And particularly, to restate the point, *it's crucial to bear in mind that Jesus is intrinsic to the one God throughout the whole process.* Because Jesus is the incarnate, Second Person of the Trinity, and because what the Son experiences the Father and the Spirit also experience, the triune God's condemnation of sin *occurs within his own trinitarian life*.

It doesn't happen to *someone else, somewhere else*.

Rather, the triune God draws the darkness and brokenness of the world into his own inner life, and it breaks him. "My God, my God, why have you forsaken me?" (Mark 15:34).

But how can Jesus—if he *is* intrinsic to the one God—say that? What sense can we make of it?

This was the deal. They'd make a world of immense beauty and joy—and, particularly, it would be *free*. It would be free to love and to sow beauty; and it would be free to hate and to sow corruption. But if it did, if it sowed corruption, what would the one God do? Would he give up on the dream of a world free to love, to create, to dance?

No.

But this kind of world would cost, and who would pay? The one God himself would pay. He'd deal with the corruption. He wouldn't let someone else, somewhere else, be destroyed by its brute and horrific force. Rather, he'd lure it outside of the city, away from the people, onto himself—into his own inner life.

And its horrific force, so contrary to his nature, would break him.

There would be a kind of fracture, if for the first time and if only for a short while, within his own life.

The loving father would lose his beloved son.

The beloved son would lose his loving father.

The Spirit would lose them both.[3]

"My God, my God, why you have forsaken me?" (Mark 15:34).

But it would give birth to a new world: "As far as I am concerned, I will never boast in anything except the cross of our Lord Jesus the Messiah, through which—as far as I am concerned—both I and the universe have been crucified. So neither circumcision nor uncircumcision matters but a new creation" (Gal 6:14–15).

---

3. God's nature, of course, is ever impassible. The preceding lines, therefore, participate in the Bible's own theologically accommodative language, language that has its own truth to tell.

Heaven, Hell, and All That

For Mike, who sees the point.

THIS CHAPTER WILL NO doubt be among the most controversial of the book. Here we come to the question of "eschatology." Eschatology derives from the Greek words *eschatos* and *logos*, essentially meaning "doctrine of the last things" or "doctrine of atonement, final judgment, and the ultimate future of all things"—or, in somewhat more traditional if misleading language: "heaven, hell, and all that."

This is what I hope to accomplish in this chapter: (1) to challenge some common assumptions about biblical eschatology; (2) to reframe certain issues having to do with eschatology; (3) clearly to present the two major and necessarily "conflicting" emphases of biblical eschatology; (4) to argue that "apocalyptic/eschatological" language, while it has a point to make, isn't designed to offer a systematic picture of the future; and (5) to present what seems to me to be the most helpful way of talking about biblical eschatology.

So, let's start with points (1) and (2). Protology, from the Greek words *protos* and *logos*, means "doctrine to do with the beginning or origin of all things." Relatedly, teleology, from the Greek words *telos* and *logos*, refers to the "original, ultimate intended purpose of all things." And here's the reason for introducing these big words: a person's eschatology is necessarily slavishly dependent upon their protology and/or teleology.

In other words, a person's vision of the ultimate end of all things is related to and dependent upon their vision of the original purpose of all things.

And here's the problem: if you start with an unbiblical or sub-biblical protology then you will end up with an unbiblical or sub-biblical eschatology. And this is, in fact, what most Christians have done.

If you begin with this: "An immaterial God made a material universe but mainly as a test tube in which to determine who deserved to be whisked away from the material world into a distant, immaterial heaven in order to worship forever . . ." then you will end up with the all-too-common dualism of Greek-style eschatology: "And so, in the end, we see that the name of the game was to sort potential worshippers into two camps: those who don't make the cut and, therefore, go to hell, and those who do make the cut and, therefore, go to heaven."

But is that actually the *biblical* vision?

Isn't the biblical vision, rather, about a good creator God who made a beautiful world that, under the gentle and creative stewardship of creatures made in his image and likeness, he intended to endure forever? Isn't, therefore, biblical teleology about *the whole material universe and the way in which creatures made in God's image might fill it with God's own divine and creative life?*

From this angle, we can see the fundamental way in which so much Christian thinking has "moralized" biblical teleology. The point is no longer about the grand vision of human beings participating in the ongoing creation of the world by filling that world with God's own life and creativity; that vision, rather, is shrunken down into the tiny story of personal morality: Are you, by the Spirit or otherwise, good enough or forgiven enough or whatever to exist and to worship in God's presence forever?

Now, to be clear, it's not that the Bible doesn't have a vision of human morality; it's just that, rather, in the Bible "morality" means "the character traits necessary to steward God's world God's way." In biblical teleology, morality serves the larger story of the universe:

Are you or aren't you the kind of character through whom God can steward his beautiful, ever-evolving universe?

But once we see that the point is about God's good creation, and about it being filled with his own life and creativity, we immediately see that our eschatological dualism—between "heaven and hell"—isn't especially helpful as a framework.

But if we get the teleology right then the eschatology will fall into line.

It isn't the case, however, that as soon as we start taking the Bible's doctrine of creation much more seriously we're suddenly universalists who neither believe in judgment nor in eschatological "separation" from God; it's that, rather, we recognize that the dualistic framework of "heaven and hell" isn't particularly helpful or biblical.

What we need, rather, is a much more biblical vision. (1) A good, creator God made a world of immense beauty and possibility. (2) He intended to steward the ongoing creation of this world through human beings. (3) Human beings went wrong, but God called Abraham and his family to put the world right. (4) And although Abraham's family too went wrong, God came in and as a human being, in and as a son of Abraham, Jesus of Nazareth, in order to rescue Israel and the world. (5) Jesus rescued Israel and the world through his life, death, resurrection, ascension, and outpoured Spirit. (6) And Jesus' Spirit offers to all human beings the possibility of becoming humans properly patterned after the image and likeness of God's Son and, therefore, of assuming the role over the creation that God had originally intended for Adam and Eve. (7) Through Jesus' people and in view of Jesus' return, God intends to rescue his broken world and to get his creation project back on track. Moreover, as soon as you grasp this picture, you see that the larger point of personal holiness is this: *You've got to be fit for this story, for this purpose.*

The point is that God, by the Spirit, is renewing heaven and earth and not least in and through those made in his image, who alone can walk within and breathe the oxygen of God's new world.

Biblical eschatology is not an arbitrary exercise in inclusion and exclusion: it's a program of the ever-holy, ever-loving, ever-giving God attempting to purify human beings for the new world over which they will exercise gentle dominion.

I think that's enough of points (1) and (2).

We now turn to point (3): the necessarily "conflicting" emphases of biblical eschatology.

On the one hand, the whole Bible is emphatic that what God makes God keeps, what God creates God preserves. However broken God's creation, he doesn't lose it; he gets it back.

So, on the one hand, you have the emphatic creational theology of the Bible. Here are some passages:

> For just as one trespass gave all people the verdict of "condemnation," so also one act of covenant faithfulness gave all people the verdict of "life!" (Rom 5:18)

> For God has trapped all in disobedience, precisely so that he might have mercy on all. (Rom 11:32)

> For just as in Adam all die, so also in the Messiah all will be made alive. (1 Cor 15:22)

> God wants all people to be saved and to come to a knowledge of the truth. (1 Tim 2:4)

> So the creation eagerly awaits the revelation of the children of God—for the creation was subjected to futility, not of its own will but because of the one who subjected it—in the hope that the creation itself will be set free from its bondage to decay into the very freedom brought about by the glorious children of God. (Rom 8:19–21)

The first four texts are mainly about the salvation of human beings, but the last text is about God's purpose to use "glorified human beings" as his means of rescuing and stewarding his now-broken creation. The logic of the last text depends upon the deep and rich tradition of Jewish creational theology.

Creation is good and God gets it back.

But this emphasis—the creation is good and God gets it back—*apparently* conflicts with but actually demands the other emphasis:

God judges, rejects, and condemns that which destroys his beloved creation.

There are many, many texts which could make the point but I'll just list two that are representative:

> When any of you has a grievance against another, do you dare to take it to court before the unrighteous, instead of taking it before the saints? Do you not know that the saints will judge the world? . . . If you have ordinary cases, then, do you appoint as judges those who have no standing in the church? I say this to your shame. Can it be that there is no one among you wise enough to decide between one believer and another, but a believer goes to court against a believer—and before unbelievers at that? . . .
>
> Do you not know that wrongdoers will not inherit the kingdom of God? Do not be deceived! Fornicators, idolaters, adulterers, male prostitutes, sodomites, thieves, the greedy, drunkards, revilers, robbers—none of these will inherit the kingdom of God." (1 Cor 6:1–9 NRSV)

> Now the works of the flesh are obvious: fornication, impurity, licentiousness, idolatry, sorcery, enmities, strife, jealousy, anger, quarrels, dissensions, factions, envy, drunkenness, carousing, and things like these. I am warning you, as I warned you before: those who do such things will not inherit the kingdom of God. (Gal 5:19–21 NRSV)

The second passage says in terse, summary fashion what the first passage spells out in a bit more detail. In the first passage, we see that Christians in Corinth were appearing before local, "secular" courts in order to settle various disputes among members of the Corinthian congregation. Paul thinks this is not only unfortunate—in terms of personal and corporate holiness, unity, and public witness—but that it reflects a total misunderstanding about the Christian vocation both in the present and in the future.

Christians are called to be the means by which God governs his new world: that's what the reference—oblique to many modern readers—to "inheriting the kingdom of God" is all about.

"Inheriting the kingdom of God" doesn't mean "going to heaven when we die" but "participating in God's kingdom/sovereign rule over his new world."

And Paul thinks that, because the Corinthian Christians will participate in God's rule in the future and should be anticipating that vocation in the present, it's nonsensical to take cases before secular courts.

In the second passage, from Paul's letter to the Galatians, the point is made with respect to deeply engrained habits of immorality: such folks aren't fit to govern God's new world God's way.

So, again, to restate the point: biblical eschatology isn't about the arbitrary inclusion of some people and exclusion of others.

It's about being fit to steward God's new world God's way.

God isn't good if he doesn't eventually deal with evil. God isn't good if he doesn't eventually flood the universe with his purgative and healing justice and peace. God isn't good if he doesn't—harking back to Jesus' own violent image of hands being cut off and eyes being torn out (Matt 5:27–30)—attempt to separate the good creation that he made from the wickedness that has and continues to corrupt it. God isn't loving if he doesn't eventually try to root the cancer out.

What are we to do, then, as Christians who should attempt to live in light of, and to articulate, a Christian vision of the future which holds on to *both* emphases: (1) God gets the creation back; and/but (2) God rules out everything corrupting it?

Here come the questions:

Does God simply, in the blink of an eschatological eye, save everyone at the moment of their death and/or Jesus' return (universalism)?

Does God ultimately lose some of his creatures to the self-destructive tendencies of their own "free" will (annihilationism)?

Does God, somehow ignoring the finished work of Jesus on the cross, actively punish sinners forever (eternal conscious torment)?[1]

---

1. There are nuanced ways of expressing both universalism and eternal conscious torment that come quite close to what I am proposing. Note: Some will not like how I've described either universalism or eternal conscious torment. I am self-confessedly working with caricatures here to make the point.

Or what?

To speak in broad brush strokes, there are essentially three major views (see above), all of which have strengths but none of which, I think, solves the major problems.

You have a straightforward universalism: at the point of death and/or at Jesus' return, God instantly "saves" all people.

This approach, while it has its strengths, has its weaknesses as well. It rightly emphasizes that (1) Jesus died for all people; (2) God, in his very nature, cannot stop loving the essence of what he himself made; and (3) humans aren't, in the present, properly "free"; they are, rather, enslaved to various kinds of blindness and numbness to the divine love.

But the weakness of this view—at least in how it is often expressed—lies in its radical discontinuity with the present. Many people essentially become, within the blink of an eye, completely dissociated from their former selves and from their patterns of thought and behavior. This view likewise runs the risk of sounding as though this present life is simply a test-tube experiment and at the end a switch is flipped and we're all essentially morally the same, irrespective of the "characters" we "built" in this life.

Then you have annihilationism: the view that the human creatures who participate in their own destructive dehumanization in the present might continue to do so into the future and that, therefore, though God continues to lure them and to love them, their own self-destructive habits eventually deconstruct their created humanness finally and forever.

The strength of this view lies in (1) its expression of continuity between this life and the next and (2) the welcome emphasis that it is not so much the good and all-loving God who condemns people but the "free will" of human beings which ultimately condemns them.

But this view, it seems to me, has one major weakness: it tends to work with a theology of human free will which isn't especially biblical. After all, from the biblical perspective, are humans actually "free" in the present to reject self-destructive evils and to grasp onto the love of God? No. From the biblical perspective, humans apart

---

My view is, after all, not very different from Hart, *That All Shall Be Saved*.

from Christ *have never been free*. They have always been, in Paul's language, "slaves to sin" (Rom 6). So, the annihilationist perspective runs the risk of saying that some humans never really had a proper chance to see and thus to grasp onto the love of God.

And then you have "eternal conscious torment." The only apparent strength of this view—though, of course, many would say that it has several strengths—is that it appears to take the biblical passages about condemnation, separation, and fiery judgment seriously. Actually, however, I would contend that this view takes those passages literalistically and, in the process, "futurizes" and systematizes the highly symbolic language of Jewish apocalyptic in ways that are inappropriate and unhelpful.

Moreover, this view of God ensuring the eternal, conscious, punitive torment of creatures made in his image runs the risk of ultimately erasing any serious and thoroughgoing Jewish creational theology, as well as rejecting any biblical doctrine of the cross. After all, if the cross is the place and the moment at which God decisively "condemned" (Rom 8:3) the sins of the whole world in the person of Jesus, there really is no place for purely "punitive" judgment anywhere else.

But, in the theory of eternal conscious torment, there is no ultimately positive purpose in view when creatures are consciously tormented forever.

So what are we left with?

To overcome the weaknesses of the above views, how can we articulate a biblical eschatology that takes seriously God's desire to rescue his *entire* creation but to do so not least by *purging* his entire creation—and the human beings within it—of corruption? How can we articulate this vision while (1) taking the desperate eschatological warnings and violent eschatological images of Scripture seriously; while (2) expressing continuity between this life and the next; while (3) realizing that, in this life, humans aren't "free"; and while (4) never losing sight of the finished work of Jesus on the cross or the ever-loving character of the true God?

We are left, I think, with what I call eternal conscious love.

Jesus and his cross dealt with the whole world's sin once and for all. There's no place for punishment for its own sake in the postcrucifixion world.[2] And the symbolic, apocalyptic images of eschatological fire (hell, Hades, etc.), of eyes and hands being separated from bodies, of torment, etc., properly point to the good and glorious day when, at Jesus' return, the all-loving God will pour out his presence upon the whole universe in full measure.

This loving, purifying holiness of God—which is simply an angle of vision on the dimension of love which burns up that which keeps us from flourishing—is often depicted as an all-consuming fire (see especially Exod 3:2 and 1 Cor 3:10–15).

This "fire" will be experienced by *all* (so 1 Cor 3:10–15).

Those more familiar with the heat, so to speak, will experience less "pain"—though not, I think, physical pain.

Those less familiar with the heat will experience more "pain" and "discomfort," as though their very selves were being attacked by the flames; it is actually that, however, the flames are attempting to destroy their fake selves so that their true selves might be manifest for the first time.

But it is the same fire, the same flame, the same purpose: God intends the whole universe to share in his own life, his own inner identity, his very own divine existence.

But it takes a certain kind of being to live that kind of life, a kind of being which has passed through the flames.

But for others, for those who reject the purpose of the flames, for those who persist in self-destructive habits, it will be a kind of torture, the torture that happens when the desperately loving and healing God meets the determinedly self-destructive habits of human beings.

And, you see, this God will never give up on them: that flame will burn and burn.

But it's not eternal conscious torment, at least not in any traditional sense.

It's eternal conscious love.

And that love is not hell-bent but heaven-bent, as it were, on the holistic rescue of creatures made in God's image.

2. I would further argue that there's no place for punishment for its own sake in God's world at all.

Eternal conscious love has its heart unshakably set on universalism on the other side of universal holiness, a holiness toward which the God of love is willing eternally to strive.

Indeed, he can do no other, because he is love (1 John 4:8).

Discipleship

For Stan, who loves the commission.

WE'VE FINALLY COME TO a topic to which you would have thought we would have come much earlier in this book. What is a "disciple?" And what is "discipleship," at least in the Christian sense?

Of course, on the one hand, we have the biblical evidence to consider. But, on the other hand, we have roughly 2000 years of this evidence's varied application to consider as well.

The word *disciple*—in the Greek of the New Testament, *mathētēs*—never occurs in the Old Testament. It was well known, however, in the wider Greek world surrounding the New Testament. And in that world it essentially meant "one who is committed to a particular teacher's teachings and pattern of life." Of course, it's related to the Greek word *manthanō*, which means "to learn," but a *mathētēs* was much more than a "learner" in our modern sense.

After all, for us moderns, we naturally separate "learning" and "behavior," the "head" and the "heart," "information" and "ethics." One can learn something and be fundamentally unchanged at the level of deep motivations and moral directions. One can intake information into the head and the body and yet have actions be unchanged.

That is not the way, however, the word *disciple* was used in the ancient world. In the Gospels, as in Plato's writings, a disciple is one who is holistically committed to a person and/or pattern of life. There's no part of the person exempt from the discipleship. And, of course, in the New Testament, all of this language is focused on Jesus himself. The statistics in this regard are striking. The word *mathētēs* occurs in Matthew seventy-two times, in Mark forty-six times, in Luke thirty-seven times, in John seventy-eight times, in Acts twenty-eight times, *and then not one more time in the rest of the New Testament.*[1] I will return to this point below.

Furthermore, in the Gospels and Acts, the use of the word *disciple* should be understood in relation to the presentation of Jesus as, among other things, a leading rabbi with a particular vision of what it meant at that moment to be the people of God. In other words, in the Gospels and Acts, a disciple is a person who has committed their entire being (and, in some cases, family)—in prayer, in Scripture reading, in sacrifice and service—to Jesus and to his vision of what it meant at that precise moment to be Israel, to be God's people.

In this connection, we've already said plenty about Jesus' vision. The good God had made a good world and had placed Adam and Eve within it to steward it on his behalf. But the whole thing went terribly wrong. So God called Abraham and his family to be his means of putting everything right. But Abraham's family, Israel, also went wrong, breaking God's covenant by worshipping other gods. So God came himself, in and as a human being, in and as an Israelite, Jesus of Nazareth.

But what was Jesus' vision and vocation, in relation to which alone we can hope to understand what it meant and what it means to be his disciple? As we've already considered, Jesus saw it as his vocation (1) to announce God's coming rescue both (a) as a coming reckoning of and judgment upon the world's sins, and (b) thereby as the world's coming salvation; and (2) to embody that message by drawing the sin and brokenness of the world onto himself so

---

1. The verbal form, *mathēteuō*, "to make disciples," occurs three times in Matthew and one time in Acts.

that it could be dealt with right there and so that the world could thereby be saved.

That's the message and mission of Jesus: to be the place where sin, brokenness, and pain are dealt with and God's love and grace are mediated and dispensed.

And that is, by necessary inference, the vocation of Jesus' disciples.

Of course, on the one hand, Jesus took *their place* too. So it's not the role of a disciple to provide the climactic death that will result in the climactic victory over the sins and death of the whole world.

But there's also a mysterious and scary sense in which disciples *do* share in Jesus' unique vocation.

> Whoever does not pick up his cross and follow me cannot be my disciple. (Luke 14:27 NRSV)

> Now, I rejoice in my sufferings, which are on your behalf, and I fill up what is lacking in the sufferings of the Messiah in my own flesh, on behalf of his body, the church. (Col 1:24)

This doesn't mean that Jesus' death wasn't unique and/or that it wasn't the decisive, climactic, one-off victory over sin and death.

Of course it was.

But it does mean that Jesus' disciples, as those who fully and completely share in his mission, are to be places where the pain and brokenness of the world meet the healing love of God.

More could be said, of course. We're also called to follow Jesus in many other areas as well. Perhaps the overarching challenge is to follow him into his commitment to give his life not just to those genetically connected to him, not just to those he liked, but to the whole world:

> Whoever loves father or mother more than me is not worthy of me; and whoever loves son or daughter more than me is not worthy of me. (Matt 10:37 NRSV)

> You have heard that it was said, "You shall love your
> neighbor and hate your enemy." But I say to you, "Love
> your enemies and pray for those who persecute you."
> (Matt 5:43–44 NRSV)

In other words, Jesus is challenging some of our most fundamental instincts, the instincts that tell us to take care of ourselves,
our own "blood," and those we most like. Jesus is inviting us into a
larger vision, not just of the world in which we live but of our own
hearts and lives. There is enough room, he's saying, for everybody.
You don't have to draw lines for who's in and who's out, as though
our main objective here were to acquire as many of the world's limited resources as possible.

Jesus is calling us to reject the illusion of scarcity, the illusion
that there isn't enough love, joy, hope, money, food, and clothes to
go around: "Give to everyone who begs from you, and do not refuse
anyone who wants to borrow from you" (Matt 5:42 NRSV).

And in this way, we are also called to give our lives and resources to the most vulnerable (Matt 25).

To say it again, we are to reject the illusion of scarcity.

There's enough love.

There's enough joy.

There's enough peace.

There's enough hope.

There are enough resources.

There are plenty of good seats at the table.

But one of the most interesting things about the "discipleship"
language of the New Testament is that *it completely drops out after
the book of Acts*. Why would that be? After all, we know that discipleship—in terms of following the pattern of Jesus' life and en-
couraging others to do the same—continued. And it continued not
least because this was one of Jesus' last commands to his disciples:
"All authority in heaven and on earth has been given to me. Go
therefore and make disciples of all nations, baptizing them in the
name of the Father and of the Son and of the Holy Spirit, and teaching them to obey everything that I have commanded you" (Matt
28:18–20 NRSV).

So, if this was one of Jesus' last commands, and if, therefore, "making disciples" continued in the life of the early church and does and should continue today, *why doesn't the language appear at all in any of the letters of the New Testament?* Why doesn't Paul say, for example, "to the *disciples* of Christ Jesus in Philippi," rather than "to the *saints* in Christ Jesus in Philippi" (Phil 1:1)? Why doesn't Paul say "to the *disciples* of Jesus in Corinth" rather than "to the *church* of God in Corinth" (1 Cor 1:2)? Why do the early church letters—the letters of the New Testament—constantly refer to the Christians as "brothers and sisters," "saints," and "the church," *but not once as "disciples?"*

There are, I think, a couple of important reasons for this, and the contemporary church would do well to bear them in mind. (1) From the very beginning, the language of "discipleship" was inextricably linked with Jesus as the sole Lord/master/rabbi. In this sense, only *Jesus* had disciples; after all, only Jesus was the Lord/master/rabbi. Of course, to be clear, Jesus himself commissioned his disciples to make more disciples (Matt 28:18–20). But these were to be, in the strict sense, ultimately disciples of *Jesus*, and not, for example, disciples of Peter or Paul.

(2) Clearly the early church, insofar as it is reflected in the letters of the New Testament—none of which use the language of "disciple/discipleship"—preferred other language and attendant connections. This is not to say that Paul, for example, objected to "discipleship" language. I very much doubt that he did. But it *is* to say that he seems to have preferred the language of "brothers and sisters," "saints," and "the church." Why?

It's crucial to see that all of this language is connected and that it represents a coherent theological vision. As we've already considered above, the language of "discipleship" evokes a particular conception: one rabbi/teacher guiding one disciple/student. And that makes a lot of sense when that one authoritative teacher is still around making/leading disciples. But what about when he's gone? He is, of course, not "gone"—he accomplished what he came to accomplish; that part of the story is over and so he's been exalted into heaven and he's poured out his Spirit. Indeed, he said that it would be better this way; he would, in a sense, be closer to us than he could have been otherwise (John 16:4–11).

But he wasn't walking around Palestine making disciples anymore. Rather, he had been exalted into heaven and had poured out his Spirit, establishing a multithousand-person community in a single day (Acts 2:41–42). What was this supposed to look like? Where were they in the story now?

And to see the point, as I've said again and again, you have to know the story.

The creator God made a world—and Adam and Eve within it as his "images"—in view of the day when he himself, in the person of his Son, would come here to make it his home. The immaterial, impassible Creator would become one with his creation, in and as a human being—that was part of the point of making humans in and as his "images" in the first place. So when this God made the world, and not least human beings within it, he was making for himself a home. Or, in the language of the Bible within its ancient context, he was creating for himself a *temple.*[2]

But this God is unfathomably holy. So when Adam and Eve sinned and thus had become unholy, not only they but also their surroundings had become unfit for God's holy presence. This could no longer be God's home, however much he wanted it to be. His holiness—because of its all-consuming love, and not for any other reason—would necessarily consume this broken place. And so, having called Abraham and his family to be his means of rescuing the world, and having rescued that family through the exodus, this God gave Moses instructions about how to build for him a little home (the tabernacle) in view of the day when he would make the whole universe his home, which had been the plan from the beginning.

But Israel, too, sinned and thus became unfit, along with their tabernacle/temple, for God's holy presence. So this is what God's been looking for all along: some people, somewhere to call his home.

And he found that in Jesus (see especially John 1:14). But the plan was ultimately to make the whole universe his home, and all

2. On this, see especially Beale, *Temple and the Church's Mission.*

human beings within it. Thus, as indispensable as Jesus' time was on earth making disciples, this was in a sense a *temporary* dispensation. It was a part of the plan, but it was a unique, time-limited, and unrepeatable part of the plan. The *ultimate* plan was for God to fill the whole earth, and all human beings within it, with his holy presence and thereby to create a community.

And therein is part of the danger of "discipleship" language and its attendant conceptions. We have to appreciate where it belongs within the story; and we have to appreciate where we are *now*. Jesus has been raised; he's poured out his Spirit; the community has been established; and here we are.

Now is not the time to think in terms of *individuals individually following Jesus and making individual disciples*. Of course, that's part of what the church is and does. The church is a community of disciples of Jesus. But the point is that we're now working with and within a *community*. We're at a different point in the story. And the early church knew that. That's why they preferred other language.

They spoke of themselves as "brothers and sisters" because— though they ultimately came from different personal, ethnic, moral, religious, and geographical backgrounds—God had made them into one family. And this fact was represented not least in their sharing of basic resources (Acts 2:44–45).

They referred to themselves as "saints" (Greek: *hagioi*)—which is the same word for "holy person" or "holy place"—because they knew where they were and who they were in the story. In and through Jesus and the Spirit, God had established the community as his home. They were holy and so God could finally come to dwell in their midst. And through them God could spread his presence into the rest of the world.

They called themselves the "church" (Greek: *ekklēsia*) because they understood themselves to be the new "assembly of the people of God" (for example, Deut 4:10; 9:10; 18:16), particularly as gathered at and around God's temple.

In other words, they understood themselves to be in the present a microcosm of what the entire universe would be like when Jesus returned. That's the point.

Now, to return to our discussion of "discipleship" language. Obviously, it's crucial in the Gospels and Acts. And Jesus himself commissions us to keep making disciples (Matt 28:18–20). It's an integral part of the life of every individual disciple and of the church as a whole.

But we do well to remember where it belongs in the biblical story. We do well to see why the church letters of the New Testament prefer other language. And we do well to beware of two things in particular:

1. We have to be wary of whether or not some churches and some Christians don't prefer "discipleship" language over the language of the church letters because "discipleship" language can subtly imply a power dynamic: "I'm making disciples. I'm the rabbi. They're my students." There's danger that way; and it's not the way of Jesus.
2. We have to be wary of whether or not some churches and some Christians don't prefer "discipleship" language over the language of the church letters because they have a very high view of individual faith and a very low view of the church as a community.

With these concerns in mind, we go and make disciples: fellow learners and fellow followers of Jesus. We're not their rabbi, and they're not our disciples. We're both, together, disciples of Jesus. And when we make disciples, we make disciples *into the community of the church*. That's where the life is. That's where Jesus is. That's where the Spirit is. And if that sounds like a very high view of the church, then it probably sounds a lot like the New Testament.

Mission and Evangelism

IN THIS SECTION, OUR first question has to be: What even *is* the mission of God? We can't, of course, share its good news (evangelism), let alone participate in it (mission), without a firm grasp of what it is. And the key to the answer comes, like everything else, within the story.

What does God want?

Is he lonely? Does he just need a relationship?

Well, no. After all, he *is* relationship, an eternal, loving, self-giving, noncompetitive relationship of love between Father, Son, and Spirit.

Does he need to be endlessly admired? Does he have a confidence problem?

Of course not.

Did he create a beautiful, dynamic, material universe within which he placed material human beings only ultimately to whisk their souls away to an immaterial heaven?

"I'll fly away, oh, glory, I'll fly away?"

Does that seem to be the story that the Bible is telling?

Well, not really.

So, the questions are: (1) what can we learn about the mission of God from locating it within the larger biblical story; and (2) what does this tell us about our mission and message as Christians embodying and sharing the good news of the mission of God?

The first point is this:

Creation is not a test tube. God was not playing a game. He wasn't thinking: "You know, what I *really* want is a host of immaterial souls hovering around and worshipping me forever and ever. But, I suppose, the best way to go about getting the best souls is to host a large and long spiritual triathlon on planet Earth. The souls of those that perform best can then come to my eternal, heavenly worship service. What those embodied human beings made of that planet—with all of the art and architecture, music and movies, dance and dining options, ballparks and businesses—was temporarily interesting but ultimately meaningless. All that ever *really* mattered was the 'condition of their souls.'"

This is, we know by now, *not* the story.

Rather, God loves creation. It was what he *wanted* to do. And he wants it to go on and on . . . forever. That was the plan.

And we can see this plan in two places in particular.

If God had ever wanted to let the physical creation go, as though it had always been a game or a spiritual test, the death and burial of Jesus would have been the ideal time and place to do that. He could have left Jesus' physical body to decompose in Joseph's tomb and whisked his soul/spirit to his heavenly throne, from which place this soul/spirit could rule the universe. But that's not what happened. God took that battered and bruised body from that tomb and raised it to fresh, glorious, and incorruptible life. In the person of Jesus, first in the incarnation and then reaffirmed in the resurrection, this God united himself to the material world he had created *once and for all*.

But this immediately raises the question: If God in Christ united himself to his creation once and for all, have we had far too low a view of the material world? Have we had far too low a view of play, exercise, work, art, music, food, handshakes, hugs, animals, mountains, rivers, trees, the sun, the moon, the stars, and the grass underneath our feet?

The biblical answer is "Yes," and one of its clearest expressions comes at the very end of the Bible. At the end of Revelation we're told that, to many people's surprise, people (or their souls) don't ascend to some immaterial heaven in order to spend eternity with God but that God himself *descends* and finally and fully takes up his eternal residence within his creation. That was, after all, the plan all along:

> Behold, God has made his home in the midst of humanity. He will live with them, and they will be his people and he will be their God (Rev 21:3)

Most Christians, sadly, have the story exactly backwards. They assume that God is longing for the day when he will finally be able to whisk us away to his abode in heaven. In this version of the story, God has always been comfortably at home where he is, in heaven, just waiting for us to show up. In this version, we're the ones longing to go somewhere else, finally to come home to God's heaven.

But that's not actually how the story works. It is, rather, *we* who've been at home the whole time, though it's not presently the home it was supposed to be. It was designed only to take on its rich and proper character when the architect himself fully took up residence. But the point is that *the architect too has been so long deprived of the home of his dreams.* It's as though he dreamed a home into existence which, for various reasons, subsequently became unfit for him and for all those presently living in it. And he's been longing to show up—and, before too long, he will. And, when he does, the home will be what he always intended it to be. It's been underneath our noses the whole time—though, to be sure, it's not presently what he intended it to be nor what it will be.

And that's the point: always to hold on to the fact that this is, yes, God's *broken* but still originally and ultimately *good* creation. He won't lose it to death and decay. He'll get it back.

There is, of course, a danger in imagining too much continuity between the present and future. And this runs the risk of underestimating the distorting and corrupting effects of sin. So, in this regard, the future will be, in the language of Isaiah 65:17, Galatians 6:15, and Revelation 21:1, a "new creation."

But there's also a danger in imagining too much discontinuity between the present and future, and this is a danger to which most modern Christians are especially vulnerable. If you're not careful, you end up suggesting that the material creation itself was at worst a mistake and at best a temporary spiritual test. And if you go this route, you end up rejecting the force of Jesus' resurrection and the ultimate hope of the Bible itself as expressed in Revelation 21–22 and elsewhere. In other words, a lot is at stake.

Let's now bring all of this home to our discussion of mission and evangelism. If the mission of God was and is to create a dynamic, beautiful, ever-evolving material universe within which he would eventually come himself to take up joyous residence with his beloved creatures, what does this tell us about our mission and our evangelism? And how can we beware of expressing too much continuity or too much discontinuity between the present and the future?

First, I want to be clear about a few things. Of course the fundamentals are still true. God perfectly loves us and wants us to learn perfectly to love him and to love others. Jesus died for us and poured out his Spirit, offering us forgiveness of sins and new and eternal life starting now. That's still true. It's still central. But there's more.

The simple fact is this: while the spiritual flourishing of human beings in relationship with God is the center of it all, that goal itself can't be fully achieved without a more holistic vision—and that's the point of the holistic vision of the Bible. God's interested in people's mental health, their relational health, their physical health, their creativity and growth, their physical, social, cultural, and political environment. God's concerned about the whole thing *because peoples' spiritual flourishing is not extricable from all of this.*

So if that's the mission—holistic flourishing—and if we're called to share in that mission in the world, what's the message? What does evangelism look like? What are we preaching/saying? What do our lives and conversations look like? If we're saying that, yes, the center of it all is a flourishing relationship with God through Christ and by the Spirit, but that this flourishing is inextricably connected *to every other area of our embodied existence*, what's the message?

Are we "Romans Road" people or "Social Gospel" people? Are we about coming into a relationship with Christ or cleaning up a poor neighborhood? Are we about salvation and sanctification, or the injustice of larger local, national, and global sociopolitical structures? Are we about personal faith or personal and public finances?

The God of Scripture is about all of this and at the same time—because it's all inextricably linked. One dimension is intricately bound up with the others. And it's not enough to think and/ or to say this purely sentimentally. It's not enough to give lip service to it in church staff meetings. Our mission and message have to embody this holistic vision at every point. In our mission and message, there's not "gospel work" on the one hand and "social work" on the other. This implies that the former has an eternal significance while the latter is ultimately meaningless, so long as people's souls are saved. But, as we've seen, that's a rejection of the entire thrust of Scripture.

Everything done in Christ and by the Spirit in God's world is gospel work. And it's gospel work because it's God's world, every square inch of space and every split-second of time.

Concluding Remarks

I HOPE YOU'VE ENJOYED this brief sketch of where "the next Christian faith" needs to go. Of course, I've essentially argued that the next Christian faith needs to be a lot more like *the first Christian faith*. That's the point. And, in particular, I've argued that we need to learn how to reinhabit the worldview of Jesus and the earliest Christians, a worldview constructed from the massive story of Scripture. Nor is this only about getting some different and interesting ideas in our heads; it's about the way in which worldview stories shape the universe and every single component of our hearts and minds within that universe. After all, in the end, good theology is about good worship.

APPENDIX

Why Care about the Creeds?

Most evangelicals spend very little time thinking about the great creeds (doctrinal statements) of the early church. But they're important, and not only for historical reasons but because of the way in which they represent a sort of theological crescendo of the movement from Scripture, through Jesus and the earliest Christians, and into some of the most penetrating, profound, and long-lasting doctrines of the Christian faith. Here we're just going to look at two moments: the Nicene-Constantinopolitan Creed and the Chalcedonian Definition. The first was finalized in 381 CE and the second in 451 CE.

THE NICENE-CONSTANTINOPOLITAN CREED

> We believe . . . in one God, the father almighty, maker of heaven and earth, of all things seen and unseen, and in one Lord, Jesus the Messiah, the only-begotten son of God, begotten of the father before all ages, light from light, true God from true God, begotten and not made, of the same nature as the father, through whom all things were made, who, for us humans and for our salvation, came down from heaven and became incarnate by the Holy Spirit and the virgin Mary and assumed humanity, who was crucified for us under Pontius Pilate, who suffered, was buried, and rose on the third day according to the scriptures, who ascended into heaven and is seated at

the right hand of the father, and who will come again in glory to judge the living and the dead, whose kingdom will have no end, and in the Holy Spirit, the Lord, the giver of life, who proceeds from the father, who is worshipped and glorified along with the father and the son, who spoke through the prophets, and in one holy and universal church built upon the apostles.

We acknowledge one baptism for the forgiveness of sins. We eagerly await the resurrection of the dead and the life of the world to come. Amen.

There are a thousand things that could be said about this remarkable statement of faith, but we'll only focus on a few high points. First, the ground and source of all reality is the one creator God. But this God is no lonely monad, no isolated despot. He is, rather, the relationship between "the one God, the father almighty," "the one Lord, Jesus the Messiah," and "the Holy Spirit, the Lord, the giver of life." There is only one God, but this God is a relationship of three persons. This is, of course, the classic statement of the Trinity.

So what? The key point is this: the ground and source of all reality is *love*, the mutual interchange of relationship.

There is no aloneness or loneliness at the heart of reality.

There is no competition or jealousy.

There is just noncompetitive interchange.

That's what God is like.

That's what the universe is like.

The other point to which I'd like to draw attention is the fact that, though this is the classic statement of the Trinity, the confession actually has a kind of fourfold structure: "We believe in . . . (1) one God, the father almighty; (2) one Lord, Jesus the Messiah; (3) the Holy Spirit, the Lord, the giver of life; and (4) *one holy and universal church.*

In other words, the church not only makes this central theological confession but herself belongs within it. She is now the central means by which the triune God is manifest in the world. Are we prepared to take the church this seriously?

THE CHALCEDONIAN DEFINITION[1]

The Nicene-Constantinopolitan creed of 381 CE features the classic statement of the Trinity: there is one God in three persons, Father, Son, and Spirit. But that didn't, of course, "solve" the problem of how to think and to talk about the now-incarnate Second Person of the Trinity. How could there be a now-also fully human being at the heart of the triune God? And, indeed, how could this divine person—the Second Person of the Trinity—have assumed humanity once and for all in the first place?

Can we really think of him as fully God and fully human *at the same time*? How could that be, and why should we care? What difference does it make?

> Therefore, following the holy fathers, we all with one accord teach people to confess one and the same son, our Lord Jesus the Messiah, the same one simultaneously complete in divinity and in humanity, simultaneously truly God and truly human, consisting of a rational soul and a body, of the same nature as the father with respect to his divinity, and of the same nature as us with respect to his humanity; like us in all respects, except for sin; begotten of the father before the ages with respect to his divinity, but, at the end of days—for us and for our salvation—begotten of the virgin Mary, the "God-bearer," with respect to his humanity—one and the same Messiah, son, Lord, only-begotten, recognized in two natures, without confusion, without change, without division, without separation; the distinction of natures being in no way annulled by their union, but, rather, the characteristics of each nature being preserved and coming together to form one person and one subsistence, not as parted or separated into two persons, but one and the same only-begotten son, the divine Word, the Lord Jesus the Messiah; even as the prophets from earliest times spoke of him, and as the Lord Jesus the Messiah himself taught us, and the creed of the fathers has handed down to us.

1. I owe some of the thoughts in this section to Williams, *Christ*.

APPENDIX

As with the Nicene-Constantinopolitan creed, a thousand things could be said about this amazingly rich, dense, and potent text. Instead, I want to focus on a few. But why should we bother with all of this tedious theological nit-picking? Does any of it really matter?

The answer is, "Yes," so let's dig in. The first point is that the full divinity of the Second Person of the Trinity, God the Son, is simply assumed. That was hammered out in the Nicene-Constantinopolitan creed and, actually, was already quite clear in the New Testament. But the question became: *How* can we affirm both the full divinity and the full humanity of Jesus without talking nonsense? How can he be *both* fully divine *and* fully human *at the same time*? Surely that doesn't work. What we must mean, so many Christians have thought, is either that Jesus is fully human but not quite fully God or that Jesus is fully God but not quite fully human.

Surely, so many have thought, it's a matter of properly balancing the percentages: 70 percent human and 30 percent divine, or 70 percent divine and 30 percent human. But he *can't* be 100 percent of both *at the same time*, right? Surely the divinity of Jesus *either* overwhelms the humanity in the incarnation—and so he's really less than fully human—or he has to "leave some of his divinity in heaven" precisely so that he will not comprise the full humanity—and so he's not fully divine, or at least not *at the same time* as he is fully human.

Or, if we are to make any sense of this, perhaps we need to think of Jesus as a kind of third thing, a mixed blend of divinity and humanity. In other words, he's neither fully divine nor fully human. But, of course, that's *not* what the Chalcedonian definition is affirming. It's affirming the 100 percent divinity and the 100 percent humanity of Jesus simultaneously and forever, "without confusion, without change, without division, without separation; the distinction of natures being in no way annulled by their union, but, rather, the characteristics of each nature being preserved and coming together to form one person."

But why is this seemingly so important to the Christians behind this statement? What's at stake?

Well, quite a lot. Perhaps, for a start, as much as the "Godness" of God, the "humanness" of humanity, the distinct integrity of God and creation, and the efficacy of salvation itself.

Here's the way it works. If Jesus is not truly and fully divine, sovereign over and within creation, then there's no particular reason to think that, when he comes to creation, he will be able to save it from the mess into which it's gotten itself. But, if Jesus is not *simultaneously* fully human, then there's no particular reason to think he'll be able to "communicate" his saving work as God to true humans. He has, rather, to be the true meeting place of true divinity and true humanity. If he's less than truly God, he can't save us. If he's less than truly human, he can't mediate God's salvation to true humans.

That's also why the divinity cannot undergo change of any kind. If there's change then there's development. And if there's development then something is necessarily either getting better or getting worse. And God—if he is God—cannot get better or worse. If he gets better, then there was something conceivably better than him; and so he is not God, at least in the Christian sense. And, if he gets worse, he, of course, cannot be God in this case either. This doesn't mean he can't be powerfully and empathetically present in our joys and in our sorrows—indeed, he is more present to them than we ourselves are. But it means that, because he is perfect, he necessarily cannot undergo development or change in that sense. That's what makes him God, able to create, sustain, and ultimately rescue us.

But, if his full divinity had somehow overwhelmed his humanity in the incarnation—such that the latter became less than a full and true humanity—then he couldn't save us *as humans*. In this case, it would mean that when the true God comes to humanity in order to save it, he cannot truly save it as such—he can only come to it and save it insofar as it *ceases* to be truly human. And in this case, it would mean the God of creation cannot fully and finally realize the ultimate goal of creation: for his true and full self to truly and fully dwell in and with true and full human beings.

The divinity must retain its full integrity. The humanity must retain its full integrity. And in this Jesus must be the saving ground of our humanity as well. The God-man, truly God and truly human, is the sign and means of our full humanity's full participation in the full divinity of the Holy Spirit. The Holy Spirit is truly and fully divine. And when we are fully suffused with that Spirit in God's new world, the Spirit won't need to shrink back from his full divinity to commune with us. He won't need to be less of himself. Nor will he make us less of ourselves—as though close communion were only possible when and where one denies themselves to make room for the other.

And this brings us to one of the profoundest truths about Jesus, who is in himself the clue to reality. At the heart of reality is the truth, in relation to which so much of our broken reality tells a lie: and the lie is that life is fundamentally constituted by "zero-sum" competition. There's not enough space, room, power, love, life, money, resources, etc. for everyone. If we are to live together it will necessarily involve competition. There will necessarily be winners and losers. We can't all be fully ourselves, together, simultaneously, all the time.

But that's what Jesus himself, in his own person, affirms. That's the deep truth he tells about the universe, about God, about humans, about creation.

There is no fundamental competition.

It's an illusion.

We can come together.

We can be fully ourselves together, at the same time, all the time, forever, "without confusion, without change, without division, without separation; the distinction of humans being in no way annulled by their union, but, rather, the characteristics of each being preserved and coming together to form one communion."

Bibliography

Beale, G. K. *The Temple and the Church's Mission: A Biblical Theology of the Dwelling Place of God.* NSBTB 17. Downers Grove, IL: InterVarsity, 2004.

Bell, Rob, and Don Golden. *Jesus Wants to Save Christians: Learning to Read a Dangerous Book.* New York: HarperOne, 2008.

Dreyfus, Herbert, and Charles Taylor. *Retrieving Realism.* Cambridge, MA: Harvard University Press, 2015.

Hart, David Bentley. *Being, Consciousness, Bliss.* New Haven: Yale University Press, 2014.

———. *That All Shall Be Saved: Heaven, Hell, and Universal Salvation.* New Haven: Yale University Press, 2019.

Kugler, Chris, and Jason Shepperd. *Reading the Bible Well.* Eugene, OR: Cascade, forthcoming.

McGilchrist, Iain. *The Master and His Emissary: The Divided Brain and the Making of the Western World.* New Haven: Yale University Press, 2009.

McKnight, Scot. *The Blue Parakeet: Rethinking How You Read the Bible.* Grand Rapids: Zondervan, 2008.

———. *The King Jesus Gospel: The Original Good News Revisited.* Rev. ed. Grand Rapids: Zondervan, 2016.

McKnight, Scot, and Dennis R. Venema. *Adam and the Genome: Reading Scripture after Genetic Science.* Grand Rapids: Brazos, 2017.

Taylor, Charles. *A Secular Age.* Cambridge, MA: The Belknap Press of Harvard University Press, 2007.

Williams, Rowan. *Christ: The Heart of Creation.* London: Bloomsbury, 2018.

Wright, N. T. *After You Believe: Why Christian Character Matters.* New York: HarperOne, 2010.

———. *The Challenge of Jesus: Rediscovering Who Jesus Was and Is.* With a new Introduction. Downers Grove, IL: InterVarsity, 2015.

———. *The Day the Revolution Began: Reconsidering the Meaning of Jesus' Crucifixion.* New York: HarperOne, 2018.

———. *The Last Word: Beyond the Bible Wars to a New Understanding of the Authority of Scripture.* New York: HarperCollins, 2005.

————. *Simply Jesus: A New Vision of Who He Was, What He Did, and Why It Matters*. New York: HarperOne, 2011.